Ghosts of Pocahontas, Virginia and Hauntings of the Appalachia's

Rodney Shortridge

Edited by Ronda L. Caudill, PhD

Copyright © 2020 Rodney Shortridge

All rights reserved. No part of this book may be used or reproduced in any manner whatsoever without written consent from the author.

Published by Full Moon Publishing, LLC

ISBN: 978-1-946232-39-7

RODNEY SHORTRIDGE

DEDICATION

The memory of my dad Verlin Shortridge. Without him I would not be the man I am today.

The memory of my uncle Allen Gross, who opened my eyes to the paranormal world.

The memory of my friend Tom Childress, who taught me so much about the history and people of Pocahontas, Virginia.

The memory of my friend Nathan Rasnick, who taught me so much about photography and was a great paranormal investigator.

The memory of my friend David Belcher, who taught me so much about second chances and was a great paranormal investigator.

CONTENTS

	Acknowledgments	i
1	Pocahontas, VA	1
2	Hebrew Bryant Cemetery	21
3	Barter Theatre	28
4	Lake Shawnee Amusement Park	35
5	Major Graham Mansion	46
6	Historic Molly Tynes Home/Stiltner Home	60
7	Undisclosed Location (Anonymous)	70
8	Ramsey School Building	76
9	Mayhew Home	84
10	Patton Crosswhite Post 6975 VFW	89
11	Nickerson Snead House Museum	97

ACKNOWLEDGMENTS

BDPS current and former members, advisors, honorary members, and friends. Allen Gross, Robyn Dalton, Jerry Conner, Jeff Dalton, Scott Osmundson, Nate Wheeler, Rayna Bentley, Breonna Fuller, Charles Clevenger, Dave Horn, David Belcher, Heather Lamantia, Jason Kwun, John Belcher, Joshua Fuller, Kim Long, Krissie Cline, Matt O'Quin, Matthew Pennington, Melinda Jackson, Micki Nelson, Mike Brown, Nathan Rasnick, Nicole Gillespie, Olivia Compton, Pat Belcher, Rev. Russ Hatfield, Aaron Shortridge, Samantha Hull, Teresa Dillon, Tina Kwun, Tracey Pennington, William Rash, Clayton Trout, Dr. Shari Stacy, Sheriff Brian Hieatt, Tazewell County Sheriff's Office and Hollywood Actress Maritza Brikisak

Pocahontas VA:
Former Mayor Anita Brown
Former Mayor Adam Cannoy
Mayor Ben Gibson
Town of Pocahontas
Historic Pocahontas Inc.
Pocahontas Town Council
Tom Childress
Amy Flick
Dakota Lee Shortridge

Barter Theater
Lake Shawnee
Major Graham Mansion
Historical Molly Tynes Home
Ramsey School Building
Dr. Mayhew Home
Patton Crosswhite Post 6975 VFW
Nickerson Snead House Museum
Ronda Caudill PhD
Dr. Terry Mullins

INTRODUCTION

The town of Pocahontas in Tazewell county, Virginia is rich with history and with hauntings. To Rodney Shortridge and his paranormal team, Black Diamond Paranormal Society, Pocahontas is like home. Having investigated the historic buildings and led ghost walks for the public, they have seen and experienced many unexplained phenomena.

Rodney's journey began long ago. As a teenager he began to hear and see things that he could not explain. Once he was followed through the woods by a man that I did not know. When he told his father, his father instructed him to ask the man what he wanted. So the next time he saw the man he asked what he wanted and then he just vanished in front of Rodney. After his grandfather Will Shortridge passed away he saw him walk past him at his grandmother's house. Rodney promptly left and went home.

After Rodney's grandmother Bertha Shortridge passed away in 2007 his uncle Allen Gross played some EVP's for him. He told Rodney that family members had shared some of Rodney's stories with him. Rodney's uncle sparked the idea to start a paranormal group in Southwest Virginia. Rodney spent that winter researching and advertising for like-minded people to join his team. After interviewing a variety of people he had the first BDPS member, Robyn Dalton. They conducted a couple of investigations with his uncle Allen to learn the ropes. Robyn began pursuing cases for BDPS. Pocahontas, VA resident, Amy Flick, and former Mayor, Anita Brown, met with BDPS about investigating the Historic Pocahontas Cemetery. The mayor liked the team so much they were allowed to investigate other locations such as the exhibition mines. After Mayor Brown's passing former Mayor Adam Cannoy asked BDPS to investigate more locations including the opera house, town hall, and the Baptist Church. BDPS met Tom Childress who gave them the entire history of Pocahontas, VA. In 2009 he asked Rodney to become a member of Historic Pocahontas, Inc. where Rodney remained a member until Mr. Childress' passing. With Tom's help we were able to investigate the Pocahontas Fuel Building, Pocahontas Presbyterian Church, and the Hebrew Bryant Cemetery. BDPS became more involved with the community of Pocahontas. They helped out with their Coal Miners Candle Light Ceremony and the Coal Miners Reunion. Tom and Rodney discussed leading a type of haunted tour to accompany the history tour of the town. For five years BDPS did walking haunted history tours of Pocahontas, VA and had huge success. All in all BDPS spent seven years investigating almost the entire town of Pocahontas, VA.

But Pocahontas is not the only place BDPS have investigated; BDPS has investigated many historic sights rich with haunted histories in Southwest VA. This book chronicles those investigations.

Chapter 1
Pocahontas, VA

The name Pocahontas comes from the Indian Princess that in 1608 at 12 years old saved the life of captive John Smith by placing her head upon him to shield him from the impending blows of the Powhatan bludgeons and pleaded with her father to spare his life. "Pocahontas" has several meanings "Naughty One", "Spoiled Child" and "Bright Stream Between Two Hills."

"Marry Moore" and "Powell's Bottom" were alternate suggestions for the town's name when a gentleman from Philadelphia dubbed it "Pocahontas", and the name remained. The year was 1881. On June 30, 1882 the name became official when a Post Office called "Pocahontas" was established.

The Discovery of Pocahontas Coal

Pocahontas and her coal have touched the lives of many people throughout the country. Pocahontas coal has helped mold and develop our nation into the greatest industrial nation on earth.

Pocahontas had its actual beginning millions of years ago, particularly in the Carboniferous Ere in geology, when many parts of the world were covered with vegetation growing in swamps. As these plants died and subsided into the water, the water protected them from quick and complete decay. In time the vegetation gradually decomposed, giving off oxygen and hydrogen, thereby increasing the percentage of carbon in the deposit. Peat Bogs were formed which in turn were buried under increasing loads of sand and mud settling from the water over them. The vegetation matter was further compressed and through millions of years gradually hardened into coal.

The first man to discover and make mention of the great coal deposits in Pocahontas was Dr. Thomas Walker, physician, surveyor and adventurer from Albemarle County, Virginia. In March 1750 he organized an expedition to explore the territory west of New River.

Major Jed Hotchkiss of Staunton, Virginia, a civil engineer and mineralogist, brought to public attention the expedition and journal of Dr. Walker. Major Hotchkiss, after careful study, asserted that Dr. Walker and the expedition was at the present site of Pocahontas in 1750. Dr. Walker was the first man to discover and make mention of the great coal deposits in Pocahontas.

Major Hotchkiss hired Captain Isaiah A. Welch, a young engineer, to search out and investigate the coal resources in and around the town of present-day Pocahontas. In 1876 Captain Welch called on Mr. Jordan Nelson, a pioneer resident in the area, and requested to see the coal bank he had heard of in his back yard. Mr. Nelson was perhaps the first to use the vast coal resources in the operation of his small blacksmith shop; he also sold the coal by the bushel to his neighbors who would pack it away on mule and horseback. Captain Welch explained to Jorden Nelson how Major Hotchkiss wanted to find natural resources in an effort to help rebuild Virginia since the War Between the States, "Civil War", was over. Mr. Nelson agreed and showed Captain Welch the vein of coal behind his house that was thirteen feet thick, the same vein that would yield a total of over forty-four million tons of coal before it would be exhausted years later.

Jordan Nelson died in 1922 at the age of 94.

Pocahontas Presbyterian Church

The Pocahontas Presbyterian Church was organized on October 28, 1891. In 1892 construction started and was completed 1 year later. The interior of this church is an example of an old congregational church with no decoration. Its design is simple but beautiful. There is no altar, only a pulpit, and the pews go from side to side with no center lanes the reason for this is so there can be no processionals.

By the late 1950's the size of the congregation had sharply decreased. In January 1970, this church was dissolved and the Greenbrier Presbytery made it a property of the Bramwell Presbyterian Church. In 1982, the Bramwell Presbyterian Church deeded the property to Historic Pocahontas, Inc. Starting in 1992 Historic Pocahontas, Inc. (HPI) received funding administered by the Virginia of Historic Resources to restore the church.

H.H. Hawes was the first pastor 1892-1904. The photography on the wall at the back of the church is of "Pastor Moore" he was the pastor 1897-1899.

Black Diamond Paranormal Society's Investigation of the Pocahontas Presbyterian Church

BDPS was asked by Tom Childress to conduct an investigation. On March 27, 2010 the BDPS team set up and the results of that investigation were captured photo evidence of unexplained shadows, red mist, and blue light streaks.

Many EVPs were captured they were as follows: a child's voice that was undistinguishable, a female voice saying, "Hey" and "Rodney". They caught an older female voice saying, "Saved", and a male voice saying, "That's hot". Also, they captured an unexplained knock.

There were other phenomena captured as well. Shadows, mist and unexplained blue and red light streaks with the photographic and audio evidence captured.

Log Cabin & Christ Episcopal Church

The Christ Episcopal Church was organized in 1884 as a mission of Pulaski Parish Church, Mr. C.H. Clark gave a tract of land for the erection of a church and parish school. Oak trees were cut down to clear the land and the larger logs were sawed into lumber for construction of the church and the smaller ones were used to build the log schoolhouse. Before 1884 there was no schools located in town. By 1887 there were 30 children enrolled in the parish school.

In 1912 the church was made smaller by being "sawed in half" and moved to its presented location, the other half of the church is located in Wise County Virginia. At that time the log cabin school was made into a rectory "parsonage". The log cabin, which was the first school in Pocahontas, was built in 1884 it was operated by the Episcopalian Church. It was sold in the 1990's.

Pocahontas Post Office

The present location of the Pocahontas Post Office is not the original location at this time the location has been undetermined.

Pocahontas War Memorial

The Pocahontas War Memorial was erected after World War II to list the fallen town soldiers.

Pocahontas Fuel Building

This building was dedicated in October 1942 and became the general headquarters of the Pocahontas Fuel Company, Inc., which was the second largest producer of bituminous coal in the world during the 40's and early 50's. During that period, around 150 people worked in the building. In 1958, the Fuel Company merged with Pittsburgh Consolidation Coal Company. However, the name Pocahontas Fuel Company was kept for this division until it was dissolved in 1980.

This building remained a division headquarters for Consolidation Coal until 1983. In 2004 all operations ceased and the building was given to Historic Pocahontas, Inc.

In the 1970's a man named James Floyd Harmon was shot to death by a town officer, Ben Wright, on the first floor near the water cooler, Wright and Harmon had run ins in previous years. Wright had arrested Harmon on several different occasion on different charges such as malicious assault on an officer, brandishing a deadly weapon and a gun battle between Mr. Harmon and another town resident from St. Clair Street to Center Street.

There is a "V" that is carved by the first-floor steps and it is claimed to be "V" for victory after World War II.

Black Diamond Paranormal Society's Investigation of the Pocahontas Fuel Building

BDPS was asked by Tom Childress to conduct a paranormal investigation within the building. BDPS investigated the fuel building on June 27, 2009 and August 21, 2010 along with a public investigation on October 19, 2013. These are the results of those investigations.

There have been many reports of shadows roaming the hallways at night, doors opening and closing on their own, sounds of footsteps, and unexplained voices when no one else is in the building also lights turning themselves on and off with no explanation.

In the area where Mr. Harmon had been killed, the K-2 meter along with the EMF (electromagnetic field) detector, kept giving high EMF readings in an area about 4' wide x 15' long and about 3' off the floor. Also, a shadow was caught on video by one of our static cameras that was placed to record in the area were Mr. Harmon was killed. Mike Brown took this evidence to Jerry Conner (Media Services Technician) at Bluefield State College to analyze this footage. Mr. Conner could not explain this event with all of his experience, technical skills and equipment.

An unexplained figure or apparition was captured moving toward the bottom right of the camera on the second floor. This figure seems to be moving the camera. There was unexplained slight movement of the camera on the second floor throughout the investigation. This happened once while Rodney Shortridge and a past BDPS member were monitoring the cameras. Rodney went out to check the camera and there was no apparent reason for this movement. He checked the camera and found that it was stable and locked in place.

There were many EVPs captured here as well. On the first floor the sound of a gunshot was captured on audio recordings. On the second-floor audio recordings were captured of an unexplained whisper saying, "OK", a metallic sounding voice making an undisguisable sound and male voice whispering, "Walking". On the third-floor audio recordings were captured of two unexplained whispers that were undistinguishable. Also, Rodney was getting a response to knocking; Rod knocked out shave and a haircut on the wall and got a response. Microcassette recorder carried by a member of the team caught an unexplained female voice saying, "Right".

Pocahontas Company Store

The Southwest Virginia Improvement Company built The Old Company Store in February of 1884. This was the first company store erected in the great Pocahontas Coal Fields. On the first level was the company store and on the upper levels were ample space for mining offices. Furniture and store equipment were installed, and the building was occupied on the first of March.

The store hosted a variety of staff including: store clerks, salesmen, junior salesmen, milliner, dressmaker, janitor, porter "a person employed to carry luggage and other loads", especially in a railroad station, and teamsters "a driver of a team of horses or mules".

The company store provided a convenient place where coal mining families could purchase meat, groceries, and clothing, furniture and mining supplies.

The company store was the largest in town and was stocked with a large and fashionable line of general merchandise of good quality. Coal miners could obtain credit from the company store and pay his store bill, house rent, insurance, lights, water, smithing (black smith), coal, doctor, bath house, and miscellaneous bills through payroll deductions.

All that is left of this amazing structure is the safe-tower with all 3 safes still intact.

Iron Fronts

The land to which the 3 Iron Fronts were located was purchased by Jewish businessmen. The iron fronts for the businesses were brought in from St. Louis Missouri. The owners sold dry goods in one store and a drug store in the adjoined building along with a liquor store.

Red Brick Road

The Red Brick Road was laid in 1910 the entire Center Street was bricked until parceled covered in 1960.

Maxwell House Coffee Commercial

The Executive Producer, Leslie Stark, searched eleven states before deciding on Pocahontas, VA. The 200-member cast was entirely made up of the residents of Pocahontas. The dinner scene was filmed inside of what is now Fayes Hair Salon.

Eric Ernhart from WDBJ 7 of Roanoke Virginia interviewed the cast and crew during the filming. Sherman Dudley was interviewed and recalled in the 1920's and 30's the streets always being full even up to midnight.

However, the commercial was only shown on the west coast it never aired in areas local to Pocahontas.

Dr. Ballard Building

The Ballard Building was built in the early 1920's for the purposes of housing the First National Bank of Pocahontas. In 1928 the CEO of the bank extorted enough funds from the bank to collapse the institution entirely.

Isaac T (of the "Hitmen") was a major investor and stockholder of the failed bank. The building was transferred to Isaac during the downfall of the bank. He was also a major stockholder and owner of the Bank of Bramwell. His name is listed on the deed.

The building was sold to Dr. Alexander and Dr. Straump in the early 1930's. The deed listed a 'No Use for Banking Institution' clause, stating that this building could never be utilized for the purposes of a financial institution or bank of any sorts. (The ruling on this deed still stands true today that no property owner can utilize the premises as any type of financial, banking or Holdings Company). The doctors set up their practice and became the only local/town physicians. Shortly after establishing themselves, the doctors entered into a relationship with the Pocahontas Fuel Company and became 'the company doctors'.

This was the place that all injured miners were brought. During the "black gold" boom of the Pocahontas coal mine the building was practically never closed as it was a never-ending process of attending to the sick and injured.

The building and practice were transferred to Dr. Ballard around 1940's (a well-known and respected local physician and the building's namesake) who maintained his medical practice in the bottom portion of the building and utilized the upper half as his apartment/home. After Dr. Ballard passed away the building remained unoccupied and unused for a number of years. Charles Gilmore purchased the building and was the last owner before giving to HPI. Now the building stands empty all but for the medical equipment that Dr. Ballard left behind. It is a peek into the past and a sight that is reminiscent of a cliché 'ghost town' building.

Black Diamond Paranormal Society's Investigation of the Dr. Ballard Building

BDPS was asked by Tom Childress to conduct a paranormal investigation. BDPS investigated the Ballard Building twice on May 1, 2010 and November 19, 2011.

BDPS had many experiences in the Dr. Ballard Building. During an investigation of the upstairs apartment two former BDPS member's had personal experiences both being touched at different times on several occasions along with being scratched.

The most astonishing thing to take place was the crashing sound like the roof falling in and it shook the building. However, after a complete search inside and out, nothing could be found for the cause, other things included unexplained temperature changes along with chills and goose bumps.

BDPS caught several EVPs. They caught a female voice saying, "OK", "Help me", and "Back off". They caught a male voice answering a question by Rodney—"No", "Bring it", "Yeah", "William Bork", "wow, WOW", and "Where she at?" They also caught an unexplained undistinguishable small girl's voice, an unexplained undistinguishable child's voice and a very low whisper saying, "Rodney". BDPS also captured the sound of kitchen utensils falling.

Pocahontas Old Town Hall, Court House, Jail & Opera House

The Pocahontas Old Town Hall, Court House, Jail & Opera House building was completed in 1895 to serve as the Town offices, courtroom and jail downstairs with the Opera House upstairs as a theater.

The Opera House was the first theater in the Pocahontas Coal Fields. In the boom days they had Broadway plays, operettas, and vaudeville acts. The Royal Budapest Opera and the comedy team of Webber and Fields along with actress Sarah Berrnhardt were among the most notable acts that graced the theater. In the 1920's the famous evangelist Billy Sunday preached a revival in the Opera House. In the mid to late 1930's the Hungarian

Community had a Hungarian Grape Festival in the autumn.

Because of the Great Depression in the 1930's the major entertainment events stopped.

It is well known that special trains were run from Bluefield, West Virginia to Pocahontas, Virginia to enable Bluefielders to enjoy such performances.

The theatre seats and slated floor were torn out and a sewing factory was placed in the building that closed after a short time. In the late 1940's, 50's and 60's it was closed up and not used until the early 70's Historic Pocahontas Inc. was formed and got a $30,000.00 federal grant that was used for partial restoration.

Numerous shows took place in the 70's and 80's. In 1989 the town government moved the town offices out of the building. By disconnecting all the water and heat it left the building in a bad state of disrepair throughout the years. There are hopes of obtaining grant funding at this time.

Black Diamond Paranormal Society's Investigation of the Pocahontas Old Town Hall, Court House, Jail & Opera House

BDPS obtained permission from Mayor Adam Cannoy to conduct a paranormal investigation in April 4, 2009. Mayor Cannoy also participated with BDPS during this investigation. During the pre-investigation interview they took photos and captured an unexplained light blue object and an unexplained red object within the balconies.

BDPS caught EVPs here as well. They caught a male voice saying, "Rodney" and a female voice saying, "Going up stairs to make a new white church", "Not giving up on you", "Rod", "Dad", "Rodney", "Amy". They also caught a child's voice whispering but the words were unrecognizable. And they also captured an EVP saying, "Go Up" and a voice whispering words that were unrecognizable.

Butt Coffin Company

Mr. Butt, the owner, was a veteran of the Confederate Army, he was originally a cabinet maker from Falls Mills Virginia but once the mine explosion took place in 1884 it has been said that Mr. Butt was asked by the mining company to build coffins for all the miners that perished in the mine explosion. It is also said that due to this tragic event it affected him deeply he never returned to building cabinets he spent the rest of his days making coffins.

Hebrew Church

Congregation of the Hebrew Church was founded in 1892. This church has connections to the Hebrew Bryant Cemetery.

Pocahontas Church's

The Baptist and Methodist Churches were established in 1882, the Episcopal Church in 1884, the Roman Catholic Church in 1896 and the Hungarian Reform Church and the Jewish Synagogue after the turn of the century.

Pocahontas Masonic Lodge

Pocahontas Masonic Lodge was founded in 1883 by the town founding fathers. It met in various places while the construction of the present lodge was being built. Most meetings were upstairs in the Butt Coffin Co. building.

In November 1886 they dedicated the lodge building, and it is the oldest lodge west of the Blue Ridge. Masonic meetings are still held in this original building.

Emma Yates Library

Originally a Milner Shop, the Emma Yates Library is the closest building left that resembles the Iron Fronts.

Community United Methodist Church (The Rock Church)

African American Methodists organized a congregation and built a wooden structure on this site. It was dedicated on May 23, 1887. The original trustees of the Methodist Episcopal Church (African America) were: John A. Brown, Bascomb Sinkford, John Willoughby, William F. Mitchell and Cheshire Froe (Union veteran of the Civil War).

In July 1924, at this location the Methodist Episcopal Church sponsored a Miners' Welfare Conference, which dealt with the health and injury problems of the miner's and the conditions of their families if they were injured or killed. This was significant in that this happened several years before Worker Compensation, Social Security, and Black Lung Benefits.

The minister, Rev. Arthur D. Williams persuaded Virginia Governor E. Lee Trinkle and Congressman George C. Peery (who later became governor of Virginia) to attend this conference.

This rock church, of Gothic architecture, was completed in 1930 under the leadership of Rev. Anderson Davis. In 1939 the name of the church became the Community Methodist Church and in 1968 this church became the Community United Methodist Church.

The Holston Conference of the United Methodist Church closed this church in 2003 and deeded to Historic Pocahontas, Inc. in 2007.

Black Diamond Paranormal Society's Investigation of the (Rock Church)

BDPS obtained permission from Historic Pocahontas Inc. to conduct an investigation within the church. BDPS conducted the investigation on April 18, 2009.

Numerous BDPS members had experiences one member had his shirt pulled, Rod kept having the feeling of something brushing the front of his hair, another member had something thrown at her and even felt a breeze from it. Other evidence was caught on DVR's this evidence includes, unexplained clicks, object bouncing on floor, something being moved and slammed against something in the basement.

Photo evidence shows an apparition that looks like a man standing at the pew area of the church in one of the photos taking by Robyn Belcher during the investigation.

Again, BDPS captured EVPs here. They captured a male voice saying, "Rodney" and then something undistinguishable

They also heard an unexplained phone ringing. However, they do not carry cell phones with them on investigations. They are left in their vehicles. This is a rule that is strictly enforced.

The Cricket

The Cricket was originally the Sliver Dollar Saloon. Beside of it was the Old Elkhorn Saloon they both were owned by a Jewish man by the last name Quass; sounds like (Kwoss).

Pocahontas Town Hall

The Pocahontas Town Hall was first used as the Bank of Pocahontas.

Black Diamond Paranormal Society's Investigation of the Pocahontas Town Hall

BDPS obtained permission from Mayor Adam Cannoy to do an investigation of the building. BDPS conducted the investigation on July 18, 2009. BDPS members had personal experiences during this investigation such as hearing knocking, sliding, footsteps, cold clammy spots, hair standing up on their arms for no reason and all three investigators heard a small child laugh.

EVPs caught here are as follows: "It's alright", "Hello", "Out", "Talk to her dad", "Don't go there", "No", and "Lisa". A female voice was captured saying "Rodney". And they caught unexplained whistling.

Pocahontas Train Station

The original train station was built in 1882. The new train station was built in 1901. And was located beside the car wash where a house stands.

The yellow building that once was the train station is now used as a Thrift Shop and storage for the Center for Christian Action.

Historic Pocahontas Cemetery

The Historic Pocahontas Cemetery was created due to the March 13, 1884 mine explosion in the East Mine that claimed the lives of 114 documented miners. Mr. Jorden Nelson was the man that sold the land to the coal company for the burial of the deceased miners. It was a month later that the bodies of the miners were recovered due to flooding of the mines.

The Pocahontas Cemetery was the first organized burial

ground in the Coal Fields.

The one hundred and fourteen miners were buried in the cemetery side by side. Stone makers hewn in the native tongues of Hungarian, Italian, Russian, Polish, Jewish, African American and Hebrew line the countless graves. These only further epitomize the uniqueness of the Pocahontas Cemetery for it was most unusual for people of different races and ethnic backgrounds to be buried together, especially in the South during the era. But it was fitting because in Pocahontas the people who lived close together, worked together, died together and now eternally lay together.

There were four miners that was identified after their bodies were recovered Braxton Bragg Moore, L.M. Hampton, Maxey and Davis. The pome on the headstone of Mr. Braxton Bragg Moore is read each year during the Candlelight Ceremony at the cemetery to remember the more than 114 coal miners killed in the explosion.

Black Diamond Paranormal Society's Investigation of the Historic Pocahontas Cemetery

BDPS obtained permission from Mayor Anta Brown to conduct an investigation of the cemetery. Three different investigations on September 20, 2008, August 15, 2009 and October 2, 2010.

BDPS was featured on A&E's Biography Channel "My Ghost Story" which featured the Historic Pocahontas Cemetery on December 12, 2011 these are the results of those investigations.

During the investigations a few of the team members had personal paranormal experiences. Strong feelings of being watched, hearing knocking coming from inside one of the tombs, seeing a white figure duck down behind a head stone. Also, the experience of the feeling of someone breathing on their neck and something tugging on their shirts "like a child tugging".

Sightings of a bright white orb come up over a headstone and then disappear, hearing unexplainable voices, experiences of hair being pulled, feeling several cold spots and witnessing a long white floating apparition. Photo evidence was captured of mists, apparitions and shadows.

One BDPS member experienced seeing a white figure near a tree. One member experienced a sharp pain in his back below his left shoulder blade. He describes the pain like someone had stuck a knife into his back and the pain lasted for around 10 minutes.

More EVPs were captured in the cemetery, some of which were featured on A&E's BIO channel's My Ghost Story. The EVPs caught there was a young male voice with foreign accent saying "Footo". They caught a young child's voice saying, "I push it". And a young female voice saying, "Trying to communicate".

Other EVPs were a female voice saying, "Why don't you just come over?", "It's them", "I better go now", "Please help", "Walk this way", "Why", and "Hello". They also captured an old female voice saying, "Here, what's happened? Uh..." and a male voice saying, "Wrong way".

Pocahontas is definitely very rich in history which explains its rich paranormal activity. Pocahontas never disappoints any paranormal enthusiasts.

Chapter 2
Hebrew – Bryant Cemetery

Recent History

According to an article published in the Bluefield Daily Telegraph in 2009 by Bill Archer "two historic cemeteries located in Mercer County near Pocahontas, Va., were on the verge of being prepared for development by a land owner, but a local non-profit organization stepped up to take temporary ownership of the property until the deeds of the cemeteries could be transferred to the appropriate parties".

Mr. Childress, treasurer of Historic Pocahontas Inc., presented the situation to fellow board members at the board's regular meeting, stating that although the eight-acre tract of land that served as two cemeteries — one plot of land used as a Hebrew cemetery for 15-20 years, and a larger section of land that was used as an African American cemetery called Bryant Memorial Cemetery should have been tax exempt. However, the land remained on the Mercer County tax rolls and had been sold at least twice for back taxes.

The most recent buyer hired a local contractor to clear the land. The contractor removed sections of 100-year-old wrought iron fence around the Hebrew section of the cemetery. A local man who lived near the cemetery, Terry Collins, informed the contractor he was stripping a cemetery. Mr. Collins then locked the gate to the cemetery and called Mr. Childress. Mr. Childress called David Katz, a Bluefield attorney who is also treasurer of Congregation Ahavath Sholom, a Jewish congregation in Bluefield.

These three men spoke with Mercer County Assessor Bill Blankenship, "who determined that the original property owner, Isiah Johnson, as well as his heirs had failed to properly deed the cemetery as a cemetery." The developer wanted to ensure that the property back into the hands of the appropriate parties. However, he also wanted to make certain that the cemeteries went to a non-profit entity.

At a specially held board meeting to determine the fate of the cemetery Katz presented his concerns and the board unanimously voted to temporarily hold the deeds to the cemeteries until the appropriate parties could receive the deeds.

Investigation

On August 29, 2009 the BDPS team (comprised of Rodney Shortridge, Mike Brown, Amy Flick & Samantha Hull) investigated the Hebrew – Bryant Cemetery located in Mercer County in the town of Coopers, West Virginia. They were granted permission to investigate by Tom Childress. The first team consisted of Amy and Rodney. The second team consisted of Mike and Samantha. The investigation began around 9:00 p.m. and finished around 11:30 p.m. This was a short investigation due to weather.

Equipment used at this site included 6 DVR's (digital voice recorders), 1 microcassette recorder, 4 digital cameras, 1 K2 meter, 1 EMF meter and 1 laser thermometer. When investigating BDPS always tries to place the DVR's in areas that have reports of paranormal activity or areas of interest in hopes of capturing audio evidence; Hebrew-Bryant Cemetery was no different. The microcassette recorder was held by Rodney as he and Amy investigated the cemetery.

They began the investigation by dividing the cemetery into two grids for each team. Team 1 consisted of Rodney and Amy investigating the front of the cemetery. They covered an area about 50 yards from the top of the cemetery down to the lower front near the entrance of the cemetery. Team 2 consisted of Mike and Samantha. They investigated the back section of the cemetery and covered an area about 50 yards. Each team worked on a rotation of about every two hours and each team rotated to the area of the last team. Due to inclement weather they rotated for a short period of time. This was a great experience for the entire team to be investigating such a historical area, considering the controversy surrounding this cemetery. Mr. Childress felt that the loved ones in this cemetery may have been disturbed in some way and wanted them to find any evidence that would show just cause for his concerns.

Evidence and Conclusion

BDPS captured many orbs and unexplained mist. They also captured many EVPs on their

DVR's & microcassette recorders. They captured an unexplained click, something moving around with no explanation, unexplained voices (which were undistinguishable), a whisper saying, "What", unexplained humming (when audio was slowed down sounds like someone speaking, but again undisguisable), a male voice speaking a foreign language (they were unable to interpret what was said) with female voice yelling, "Good". There was also an unexplained banging sound and a female voice saying, "Just feel better".

BDPS concluded that the Hebrew – Bryant Cemetery had low paranormal activity in the form of EVP's, orbs and unexplained mist.

Case 016 Hebrew-Bryant Cemetery 8/29/09 unexplained mist.

Case 016 Hebrew-Bryant Cemetery 8/29/09 unexplained mist.

Case 016 Hebrew-Bryant Cemetery 8/29/09 unexplained mist.

Chapter 3
Barter Theatre

History

The building that is now The Barter Theatre was originally constructed in 1831 as a new location for Sinking Springs Presbyterian Church. In later years it housed theatrical performances such as "The Virginian" which debuted on June 14, 1876. In 1890 the title was transferred to the town of Abingdon by the Sons of Temperance so it could serve as a town hall also used to be a Fire Hall. During the Civil War, the Martha Washington Inn was used as a Confederate Hospital. Since the Union would not attack hospitals, the confederates dug a secret tunnel to the Barter Theatre where they also stored ammunition. The Union secretly knew of the tunnel and shot two confederate soldiers.

Then Mr. Porterfield, a native young actor from southwest Virginia opened The Barter Theatre on June 10, 1933.

Reports & Claims

It has been reported that their spirits still haunt the Barter. Other claims are that the tunnel collapsed. After the renovation of the Theatre, the apparition of Robert Porterfield has been spotted on stage and in the balcony, which was his favorite place to sit during plays. It is also reported that prop scenery has said to have moved at night. There have been reports of the sounds of clapping and disembody voices being heard in the auditorium, dressing rooms and basement.

Investigation

On October 24, 2009 the BDPS team, comprised of Rodney Shortridge, Aaron Shortridge, Mike Brown, Amy Flick, Tina Kwun, Nicole Gillespie, Jason Kwun & Special Guest Rachel Sheppard, investigated the Historic Barter Theatre located in Washington County in the town of Abington, Virginia. They were given permission to investigate this beautiful and historic site by Master Electricians Josh Wilson, Ken Cornett, cast and members of the Barter Theatre. BDPS decided to use three teams to investigate this site. The first team consisted of Tina, Jason and Rodney. The second team consisted of Aaron, Amy and special guest Rachel. The third team consisted of Mike and Nicole. They alternated Jason and Nicole with different teams to help with their training. The investigation began around 1:00 a.m. and finished around 5:45 a.m.

Equipment used at this site included 5 DVR's (digital voice recorders), 3 microcassette recorders, 2 camcorders with night vision, 1 daylight camcorder, 4 digital cameras, 1 K2 meter, 1

EMF meter and 1 laser thermometer.

They placed 1 DVR, 2 night vision camcorders at the balcony of the theatre where it was reported by cast and employees of the theatre to have seen an apparition. They also placed 1 DVR in the middle of the auditorium section of the theatre along with 1 DVR placed on the stage of the theatre, and in addition 1 microcassette recorder carried by the team members that investigated the stage area of the theatre. BDPS also placed 1 DVR in the hidden tunnel under the theatre. They also placed 1 DVR in the "Scary Room" in the basement along with 1 microcassette recorder, and placed 1 microcassette recorder in the actors' break room, which was also carried around by each team into all the dressing rooms located in the basement. The daylight camcorder was placed in the main lobby along with 1 DVR. Each team carried along with them during the investigation one of the following: the K2 meter, EMF meter or laser thermometer.

BDPS began the investigation by dividing the theatre into three sections. First rotation started with Team One, including Tina, Jason and Rodney. They began by investigating the upper theatre area which consisted of the balcony, balcony lobby, auditorium, stage and backstage of the theatre. Team Two included Aaron, Amy and Rachel; they began their investigation in the basement that included the actors' dressing room, actors' break room. Team Three was Mike and Nicole. They began investigating in the tunnel and Scary Room, which is located, adjoined to the basement. Each team worked on a rotation. About every two hours each team rotated to the area of the last team that was investigating. A few times during the investigation they also rotated team members. This was a great experience for the entire team to be investigating such a large area along with new members. This was a huge experience and very helpful in training of the new investigators.

Evidence and Conclusion

While investigating the auditorium Tina was sitting beside one of the DVR's that was placed earlier by Rodney on a chair arm in middle of the auditorium. At the beginning of an EVP session and she used one of the techniques that BDPS uses during their investigations by knocking on something in hopes of a response. Tina asked the question "Can you knock back?" She continued to knock four times and received one knock back in response. Tina asked Rodney who was investigating in the balcony if he heard the knocking. He replied that he did not. Later while Rodney was going over all of the recordings, he discovered the knock that had responded to her knocking. This evidence was captured on 3 different DVR's that were placed on the stage, auditorium where Tina was sitting and the one in the balcony where Rodney was investigating.

BDPS captured an unexplained handprint on a window located at the balcony lobby along with what appears to be an apparition in the adjoining window from the handprint. They also captured an unexplained blue light moving above the stage and photographed unexplained orbs.

Note: BDPS does not support the idea of orbs as evidence of the paranormal because most orbs can be explained away as dust, bugs, rain, mist, fog, etc. There are cases where the orbs they photographed seemed to move with some type of intelligent intent. BDPS posted these photos because they feel that there needs to be more investigation into the Orb Phenomenon and shouldn't be quick to dismiss this phenomenon without further investigation and explanation.

BDPS also captured many EVPs. They captured the following EVP's: and unexplained noises on our DVR's & microcassette recorders: A child's voice saying, "This is fun" in the actors' break room. They also caught an unexplained breath, a male voice saying, "Who's Jason", and a female voice saying, "I know you (undisguisable words) over here".

Note: These EVP's happened within seconds of each other. Tina and Rodney were investigating the Actors' Break Room when Tina heard a heavy breath and asked Rodney if he heard it. He responded, "No. It might have been Jason." They debated as to whether or not it was Jason; they even called the other team leaders to get a location of Jason. He was on the other side of the building with Team 2 at the time of this event.

BDPS also captured evidence in the main front lobby. They caught an unexplained noise or voice. And in the auditorium, they captured the following: an unexplained and undistinguishable voice, an unexplained sound like a child giggling, unexplained movement, a child's voice saying, "Hey mommy", an unexplained and undistinguishable voice, an undistinguishable child's voice along with a Male voice whispering "Rodney".

In the Scary Room Basement, they caught EVPs of a male whispering, "Help". On the stage they caught an unexplained click, a male voice whispering, "I got to check the tapes", an unexplained noise (that sounded like a duck call), an unexplained low click, and whispering extended out saying, "O..v..e..r h..e..r..e".

There was also evidence captured in the theater balcony. BDPS caught a female voice whispering undistinguishable words, a male voice whispering extended out "I..k..n..o..w", and a musical note from a piano. *Note: there was no piano.*

BDPS have come to the conclusion that the Barter Theatre has moderate paranormal activity.

Case 017 Barter Theatre 10/24/09
Unexplained handprint on a window located at the balcony lobby along with what appears to be an apparition in the adjoined window from the unexplained handprint. They also captured unexplained blue orb moving above the stage.

Chapter 4
Lake Shawnee Amusement Park

History

The property has a rich recorded history. Beginning in the late 1700's where documentation begins with the locally known story of the 'Clay Family Massacre.' On August of 1783 at Clover Bottom (now Shawnee Lake, located between Princeton and Matoaka), in present Mercer County, there was a deadly encounter between Native Americans and white settlers. This was the murder of Bartley and Tabitha Clay, children of Mitchell and Phoebe Belcher Clay, and the capture and ultimate execution of their son Ezekial by Shawnee Indians. As told by historian Rev. Shirley Donnelly in the article, "The Massacre of Clay Children," Beckley Post-Herald, September 5, 1979, the incident unfolded as follows:

"In the month of August, Mitchell Clay had harvested his crop of small grain, and wanting to get the benefit of the pasture for his cattle, he asked two of his sons, Bartley and Ezekial, to build a fence around the stacks of grain. While Mitchell Clay was out hunting, the two sons were building fence pens around the grain stacks. The older daughter, with some of the younger girls, was down on the riverbank putting out the family washing. While this was in progress, a marauding body of eleven Indians crept up to the edge of the field and shot young Bartley Clay dead. When the girls heard the shot that killed their brother, they lit out for the house for safety. Their path to the house was directly by where Bartley had fallen. An Indian attempted to scalp the youth and at the same time capture the older girl, Tabitha Clay. She was trying to defend the body of her brother. In the struggle the girl reached for the knife which hung on the Indian's belt. Missing the knife, the Indian literally cut her to pieces before killing her."

"Ezekial Clay, about 16, was captured by another Indian. About the time of the Indian attack, a man named Lincoln Blankenship called at the Clay cabin. When Mrs. Clay saw her daughter Tabitha in her death struggle, she begged Blankenship to go and shoot the savage and save her daughter's life. But Blankenship ran away from the scene and reported to settlers on New River that the Clay family had been murdered by the Indians."

"When the savages got the scalps of Bartley and Tabitha Clay, they left the area with Ezekial Clay as their prisoner. Mrs. Clay took the bodies of Bartley and Tabitha to the house and laid them on the bed. She then took her small children and made her way through the woods to the home of James Bailey, six miles distance. Meanwhile Mitchell Clay retraced his steps homeward and discovered the scene of horror. Thinking all his family had been killed or captured; Mitchell Clay left his cabin and headed for the settlements on New River.

"A party of men under the leadership of Captain Matthew Farley went to the Clay cabin and buried the two Clay children. They then pursued the Indian party. They caught up with the Indians in present day Boone County. Several of the Indians were killed. Charles Clay, brother of the two murdered Clay children, killed one of the Indians. Ezekial Clay, the captive lad, was hurried away by the Indians who escaped the Captain Matthew Farley party and was taken to their towns in Ohio. There he was burned at the stake, the third of Mitchell Clay's family to meet an untimely death at the hands of savages." (Paul Ray Blankenship)

There is another part of the folklore and legend that surrounds the park; it is the alleged haunting of a girl, boy and/or children that died due to a mechanical swing malfunction. There is also an unknown elderly woman who was buried in an unmarked grave somewhere on the property as well.

There was an excavation that was done in the late 1980's at the Amusement Park. The dig site is known as 'Snidow - 46MC01.' According to Marshall University's Sociology and Anthropology Department confirmed by Dr. Nicholas Freidin (Marshall's Lead Archeologist) that the dig sight known as 'Snidow -46MC01' did, in fact contain human remains, pottery, fire pits, foundations to buildings and an unprecedented wealth of artifacts from the 14th century. He also indicated that there was an additional find of pre-history artifacts that have been documented.

Lora Lamarre – Senior Archeologist with West Virginia State Preservation Office confirmed that the dig was reported and recorded as, 'it contained a wealth of artifacts which included an entire village.' This dig was literally unprecedented in the number of in-tact artifacts and information that could be obtained from it regarding the Shawnee Indian Tribe.

Reports and Claims:

There have been many tragic claims at this location that have allegedly ended in death. The tragic killings of the Clay Family members history prove this actually happened. Also claims that a swing that was once near the ticket booth, that is no longer there, a truck making deliveries to the park accidentally backed up into the path of the swing, and a young girl was killed when she allegedly was struck by the delivery truck , a boy drowning in a swimming pool that was on the property many years ago, some Chicago men being killed and buried on the property, people being attacked by unseen and seen spirits as well as demons. Unexplained disembodied voices, orbs, dancing lights, shadows and apparitions which could be the un-resting spirits of the Clay Family or possible the Natives that once lived on the property.

There have been many paranormal investigations conducted on this property throughout the years with people coming from around the world and even big TV Networks featured Lake Shawnee on ABC's TV show, Top 10 Scariest Places TV Show hosted by Linda Blair. A great percentage of investigator come away from their investigations with their conclusion that this property is haunted.

The Ferris wheel that is on the property was bought and placed on the property in the 50's and from our research no one has died or been killed on this ride. The swings that are near the Ferris wheel have reports of a certain swing moving on its own for no reason and most people have the misconception that this is the swing in which the girl was killed; that assumption is incorrect. The swing that the girl allegedly was accidently killed on is no longer on the property. Also, on the property is an old rundown mobile home that Mr. White said was the hot dog stand. At the time of the BDPS investigation the area was badly flooded which made it very difficult to cover the entire park area of the property. The park is now an area for local catfish tournaments that are held on the site weekly.

Investigation

On June 18, 2010 the BDPS team investigated Lake Shawnee Amusement Park located between Princeton West Virginia & Spanisburg West Virginia. Team members were Rodney Shortridge, Mike Brown, Amy Flick, Matt O'Quin, and Heather Lamantia, with special guests Clayton Trout and Dr. Shari Stacy.

BDPS decided because of the size of the park that each team would investigate separate areas of the park and adjoining property simultaneously, while one member would watch the camera monitor in their base tent.

They began their investigation around 7:00 p.m. with a walking tour of the park that was given by Mr. White. They began to set up around 9:00 p.m. then proceeded with the investigation soon thereafter. They concluded the investigation around 6:30 a.m. the following morning. Each team worked on a rotation changing their location about every 3 hours. This was a great experience and very helpful in constant training.

Equipment used during the investigation was as follows: 9 DVR's (Digital Voice Recorders), 2 microcassette recorders, 4 zero lux low lever IR (infra-red) cameras, 2 Kodak digital cameras, 1 Nikon camera, 1 Fuji digital camera, 1 Canon digital camera, 2 Samsung digital cameras, 1 motion diction IR (infra-red) field video/camera, 2 K2 meters, 1 EMF (Electro Magnetic Field) meter, 2) laser thermometers.

They placed (1) DVR (Digital Voice Recorder) in each of the areas of the park with reports or claims of paranormal activity, including the ticket booth, abandoned mobile home (aka Hot Dog Stand) by the lake, Ferris wheel, chain link swing set and the upper end of the property away from the park. The (2) IR cameras were placed at the upper end of the property to cover the entire field, (2) Microcassette Recorders were carried by two different teams. Also, each team carried along with them during their investigations one of the following: K2 Meters, EMF (Electro Magnetic Field) Meter or Laser Thermometers.

Evidence and Conclusion

Mike, Shari, and Clayton in field where the base tent was set up – about 75 yards from tent on the road in the direction of the house trailers. There were several personal experiences. At one point Mike asks, "Will you make a noise?" Both Shari and Mike heard a noise, which is noted at about 8:01p.m. on audio 1-A-001 and noted on EVP log sheet given to Rodney Shortridge. Clayton did not hear the noise and the noise is not audible on the audio.

At about 9:30 p.m. on the audio all three investigators – Mike, Clayton, and Shari state that they heard a growl. Clayton and Mike question if it is traffic noise, but because of the location the growl seems to come from, what they determine is the direction of the highway. However, the field area of the property the 'growl' is not audible on the recording. Investigators hear murmuring coming from the direction of the tree line toward the trailers. The murmuring is not audible on recordings.

At tractor 11:10 p.m. BDPS captured the following evidence: Beginning at 1:46 a.m. into audio they began to get strong hits on the K2 meters. One K2 meter was positioned at the front of the tractor and the other K2 was positioned on the tractor seat. Both K2's received strong hits at different times in response to questions, which are audible on the recording. No EVP's were recorded on Shari's Sony recorder. At 5:25 a.m. Shari asked, "Do you want to play," which initiates the strongest hit from the K2 meter positioned at the front of the tractor.

At swings the following evidence was captured: One good hit on Mike's K2 and the camera battery drain on both Clayton's and Mike's camera. Both cameras had a full battery. Clayton's camera shut completely off several times. Battery level fluctuated on both cameras showing empty bars and then bars would show camera half charged. Members of BDPS witnessed a swing moving on its own.

Heather Lamantia had the following experiences: Heather stated, "I was teamed with Matt O'Quin for this investigation. We were walking toward the pavilion area, just asked questions at random. From across the lake, over by swings and Ferris wheel we heard what sounded like a female voice. At first, we thought it may have been Amy Flick, who was also at amusement park area. It turned out she was only just a short distance away from us at the lake when it happened. No other team members were there at the time. We aren't able to explain that."

The most memorable experience was around the ticket booth area of amusement. In front of the booth Heather began to smell 'buttered popcorn'. It would come and go and in different spots. Also, she caught the scent at the big tree just across from the booth. Right in front of booth was where the scent was the strongest.

She tried the swing test as the owner suggested. Heather held her hand about an inch over the swing that was indicated during the tour. The swing moved slightly. The chains seemed to 'twist' at that time. Matt confirmed this, he also saw it happen. No other swings moved and no breeze was blowing. No contact with the swing itself by her hand or body. It could not be explained.

There was also photographic evidence captured at the Lake Shawnee investigation. There are photos with unexplained orbs, unexplained lights and unexplained mist.

There is video evidence of a K-2 hit by one of the teams located at the swing set.

BDPS captured EVP's and unexplained noises on the DVR's and microcassette recorder. At the Ferris wheel BDPS caught an EVP of an unexplained click, unexplained voice saying, "Jeffery", and an unexplained male voice saying, "What". At the ticket booth they caught 2 unexplained knocks, a Girls laugh, footsteps, a loud click and a knock and then footsteps. At the tractor BDPS captured an EVP of a male voice saying, "Come up". And at the hot dog stand they captured a breath and a voice saying, "Hey".

BDPS concluded that the Lake Shawnee Amusement Park has very low paranormal activity. The forms of EVP's, interesting photographic orbs, unexplained lights, mist, audio evidence and personal experiences that helped them to come to this conclusion.

However, Lake Shawnee is located in a geographically unique area. The grounds are surrounded by mountains in this particular location, thus forming a bowl shape (as you can see by the map below). In this type of setting, it is typical for the bowl-shaped geography to act as an "amphitheater." This amphitheater-effect can distort the acoustics within the bowl itself. This can and does cause voices, traffic and typical everyday noises to be amplified. This, in turn, could explain some claims of disembodied voices.

Also, surrounding the park are two major highways, Routes 10 and 19. As witnessed by BDPS on their investigation, these Routes are heavily traveled at night, also explaining some of the 'unexplained lights' from previous claims. There is also a tree line and a creek that surrounds another large portion of the site, which separates the property and an adjacent mobile home park. With the combination of the amplified acoustics, the close proximity of the trailer-park and the constant highway noise, we conclude that most of the 'unexplained phenomena' surrounding this area can now more logically be explained.

As seen on the map below, any traffic, voices, sounds and lights could potentially be bouncing back from the surrounding mountains and the tree line that surrounds the park. honored to have had the success we've had and to be working alongside such a professional team.

Case 022 Lake Shawnee Park 6/18/10 Map of Lake Shawnee

Case 022 Lake Shawnee Park 6/18/10 Unexplained orbs an unexplained mist

Chapter 5
Major Graham Mansion

History

The Major David Graham Mansion has been misnamed. It should have been named the Squire David Graham Mansion in honor of the Major's father! Squire David is the original mansion owner who settled this 6000-acre estate, including 12 local iron furnaces, forge, gristmill, rolling mills, nail works, and a general store. He was part owner of the Wythe Union Lead Mine Company and served as Director of the Virginia Tennessee Railroad Company. His picture can be found on the local paper currency of the time! Located in the Graham's Forge community of northern Wythe County, the Major Graham Mansion and the Graham family's haunting yet historical story is one the best-kept secrets in Southwest Virginia.

The Family

Squire David was born in 1800. In 1770, his father, Robert Graham, emigrated from County Down Ireland to the Locust Hill area of what is now Wythe County. He served one year in the Revolutionary War and was father to seven children from his first wife, Mary Craig, and fathered eight children by his second wife, Mary Cowan. Robert Graham was a gimlet maker, preacher, and operated an "ordinary" in what was then Montgomery County. Robert Graham died when David was 10 years old. His older half-brothers, James and Samuel Graham, and their uncle, Joseph McGavock became guardians of David and his younger siblings. At age 26, Squire David purchased 2000 acres on Cedar Run Creek, and also purchased various iron-making buildings, and a furnace from the Crockett Family and John Baker. Baker's father, Joseph Joel Baker, was murdered at his cabin where the present day mansion is located by his slaves, "Bob" and "Sam" on May 6, 1784. Hanged from a hickory tree on the hill overlooking the mansion, the local lore has it that Bob and Sam still roam the hills surrounding Cedar Run.

In 1835, Squire David married Martha Bell Peirce of nearby Poplar Camp. Even though their marriage was often a stormy union, they managed to produce eight children, two of which died as infants. It is said by many locals that "the restless spirits of Martha and Squire David live on today at Cedar Run." Major David Graham was their first-born child in 1838 and lived his entire life at Cedar Run. He served as a Lieutenant in the Civil War and formed the local 51st infantry regiment with his brother-in-law, John Robinson. The Major inherited the mansion and the Graham businesses. He also managed the Graham's Forge store with Robinson. Major Graham married Nancy Montgomery Tate in 1868 and they raised eight children at Cedar Run; their children were Elizabeth "Lizzy" Graham Sanders, David Graham, William Tate Graham, M.D., Patsy Peirce Graham Sanders, Charles Tate Graham, Katherine "Friel" Graham Fulton, James Montgomery Graham, and Robert Calvin Graham. Recently discovered were dated signatures of Friel, Lizzy, and Martha on mansion walls, doors, and windows. "Nannie" Tate Graham, the descendent of a Native American chief, lived in the mansion until her death in 1921. The Graham family tree reveals that patriarch, Robert Graham is Nannie Montgomery Tate Graham's great grandfather from his first marriage and is Major David Graham's grandfather from his second marriage

Major Graham's sister, Elizabeth "Bettie" Ann Graham Robinson, kept a diary during the Civil War that reveals much about the Graham home life, including the "often dark relationship" that existed between her parents. *The Journal of Bettie Ann Graham, October 18, 1860 – June 21, 1862* is published and housed in the Special Collections Library at the University of Virginia. Seventh child of Major and Nannie Graham, Wytheville banker James "Jim" Montgomery Graham and his family, were the last of the Grahams to live in the mansion. They moved to Wytheville in the 1930s. Much of the known Graham history has been provided by Nannie Tate Graham, local historians Davy Davis and Mary Kegley, Catherine S. McConnell *(Sanders Sage, 1972),* and by Frederick "Rick" Graham, grandson of Major David Graham, who passed away in 1990.

Reports & Claims:

There have been many tragic claims at this location that have allegedly ended in death. The murder of Joseph Joel Baker in his cabin where the mansion is located today. According to court proceedings Mr. Baker was killed by his slaves. On May 6, 1784 the two slaves that were tried for Mr. Baker's murder were hanged from a hickory tree on a hill overlooking the mansion. Local legend has it that these slaves roam the hills surrounding Cedar Run to this day. They were buried in unmarked graves on the property. A clairvoyant has made claims of a woman that is described as the "women in white" that looks out the window of a room on the 2nd floor. This same clairvoyant reported to say the woman is wearing a wedding dress, but these claims cannot be verified. Some speculate she is waiting for her fiancé that may have died during the Civil War. Many people have claims of hearing disembodied voices, being touched when no one was around them, seeing apparitions, objects moving on there on, the smell of pipe smoke when no one is smoking, and so on. The list is long; this is possibly due to the mass number of visitors throughout the world that come to this historical site to have a chance to experience such an amazing place.

Investigation

On June 26, 2010 the BDPS team investigated Major Graham Mansion located in Max Meadows, Virginia. The investigators were as follows: Rodney Shortridge, Aaron Shortridge, Mike Brown, Matt O'Quin, Heather Lamantia, Nathan Rasnick, along with new members and honorary members, Micki Nelson, Clayton Trout & Dr. Shari Stacy and special guests, Nick Ferra and Kelly Warf of Virginia Paranormal Society (VPS).

BDPS obtained permission to investigate this historical site by J.C. Weaver owner of the Major Graham Mansion, Mary Lin Brewer Director of the Major Graham Mansion, and Nick Ferra of Virginia Paranormal Society. Due to the size of the mansion and with the number of out buildings, that consists of the slave house, general store, barn and the yard surrounding the property, BDPS decided that each team would investigate separate areas of the property and structures simultaneously while one team would watch the camera monitors at base camp within the mansion. The investigation began around 6:00 p.m. with a walking tour of the mansion that was given by Nick Ferra. They began set up around 7:00 p.m. then proceeded to conduct the investigation soon thereafter. Team 1 consisted of Rodney and Matt O'Quin, Team 2 consisted of Nathan Rasnick and Micki Nelson, Team 3 consisted of Dr. Stacy and Clayton Trout, Team 4 consisted of Aaron

Shortridge and Kelly Warf, and Team 5 consisted of Mike Brown and Heather Lamantia. Nick Ferra assisted different teams throughout the night during the investigation. Each team was placed in each of the buildings to investigate, with one team investigating the outside grounds surrounding the buildings, and one team monitoring cameras back at base. Each team worked on a rotation changing their location about every 2 hours. The investigation concluded around 6:00 a.m. the following morning.

Equipment used during this investigation is as follows: 9 DVR's (Digital Voice Recorders), 3 microcassette recorders, 4 zero lux low lever IR (infra-red) cameras, 1 Panasonic handheld camcorder, 1 Sony handheld camcorder, 3 Kodak digital cameras, 1 Nikon camera, 1 Fuji digital camera, 1 Canon digital camera, 2 Samsung digital cameras, 1 motion diction IR (infra-red) field video/camera, 2 K2 meters, 1 EMF (Electro Magnetic Field) meter, 2 laser thermometers.

BDPS placed 1 DVR in each of the areas of the property with reports or claims of paranormal activity: including the barn, general store, slave house. In the mansion they placed one in the children's room, attic, master bedroom, pink room, basement, and the brides' room. The 1 IR camera was placed in the attic, 1 was placed in the children's room, 1 was placed in the master bedroom and 1 was placed in the brides' room. 1 Panasonic handheld camcorder was placed in the basement and 1 Sony handheld camcorder was placed in the kitchen. 3 microcassette recorders were carried by three different teams during the investigation. Also, each team carried along with them during their investigations one of the following: K2 meter, EMF meter or laser thermometer.

Personal Experiences

While doing the tour and walk through BDPS were in Clair's room, Micki and Mike were standing at the doorway when they both heard footsteps. Mike went up and down the stairs searching but found nothing.

Micki and Nathan experienced some activity in the Brides Room. They both heard knocking that sounded like someone was in the next room (Christmas Room); this happened on a couple of occasions. That was when Nathan called Rodney over the radio and asked if they were the only ones in the house, which they were. After a while that activity stopped. As Nathan walked from the bride's room door, he got chill bumps on his right arm. He said he felt as if someone walked past him to go into the room. He took some pictures of the room from the hallway and some out in the hallway.

Heather Lamantia had two experiences that stand out on this investigation. The first experience occurred in the General Store during the first round of the investigation. She was standing at in front of the counter and Mike Brown was sitting on a wooden bench about 2 feet away. As Heather was standing there conducting an EVP session she felt a touch on her inner left ankle.

Heather mentioned this to Mike; he used flashlight and K-2 meter and detected nothing. They resumed their EVP session and she felt it again. Once again Mike saw no trace of anything and no unusual K-2 readings. He left the K-2 at Heather's feet but nothing further occurred, partially due to the fact that at some point the K2 meter had turned itself off.

During the second round of investigations Heather had a second experience. I was in the Confederate Room while conducting another EVP session with Dr. Stacy. They were both sitting on the floor on the right side of the room. They were asking questions when Heather suddenly felt a chilly breeze on the left side of her body. She asked Dr. Stacy if she felt a breeze; she did not. They resumed their questioning. Again, Heather felt this same breeze along her left side. She asked some direct questions about this chilly breeze. Heather seemed to get a response with another chilly breeze at her side. Once again they resumed their questioning, and once again she felt the breeze one last time. Dr. Stacy said she never felt a breeze in the room. The room was very stuffy, no windows open, no real way for a breeze to occur. They were unable to find a source for any breeze by natural causes.

The first experience occurred while Matt and Rodney were investigating the children's room. Matt was to the left of Rodney about 6 to 8 feet away sitting down as was Rodney. Clayton had placed a plasma ball in the middle of the room as an experiment to see if it would attract any response to the light and the energy that it creates. Matt and Rodney were focused on the plasma ball and Rodney noticed a strange faint white light. It was moving very fast and floating above the plasma ball. The light moved to the floor up the wall around the ceiling and halfway around the room before it disappeared. It moved very fast at times and slow to the point of floating at times. Rodney asked Matt if he saw the light. His response was, "Yes, what the hell is that!?" As Rodney started to move from his chair the light disappeared as fast as it appeared.

Matt and Rodney checked the entire room with the K-2 meter to see if they could find any electromagnetic field disruptions; there were none and no cold spots. Matt checked the hallway outside the door to the children's room to make sure no one was in the area with their flashlight on. There was no one in the hallway that had a flashlight that could have created what they had seen. Even light from outside was investigated and there were no passing car lights and all members were in there investigating locations. The only other members in the house were Aaron and Kelly watching the camera monitors. Rodney called on the radio and asked them if they saw anything on the camera that was located in the room; they reported back they hadn't seen anything. They could not find any explanation for the light they saw.

The second experience occurred while Matt, Nick and Rodney were in the general store investigating. While in the general store Nick was sitting behind the counter about 6 feet away and in front of Rodney, Matt was to Rodney's left about 8 feet away sitting on a bench as was Rodney. They were conducting an

EVP session, asking questions and awaiting a response to one of the questions Rodney asked, "Do you know the town or county that was once called Jeffersonville? That is where I live. It is now called Tazewell and the county is also called Tazewell." Within a few seconds of Rodney's question they got a surprised response of a growl that everyone in the room heard. Rodney replied, "So I take it you don't like the town?" Again, they heard a low growl. Matt and Nick investigated the area while Rodney went outside to check around the store to make sure there weren't any animals nearby that may have made the growling sound. Rodney investigated the outside of the building but could not find any animals nor explanation for the sound they had heard. Rodney returned to check with Matt and Nick to see if they found any evidence that could explain what they heard. They told Rodney that they also could not find the source of the growl.

Evidence

BDPS captured photographic evidence at this location. These photos were of unexplained orbs and a dark area covering a child's ball in the children's room. The video evidence they captured was of an unexplained figure or apparition walking outside by the basement door. Later, an orb can be seen that appears and disappears near the same door in the basement.

BDPS also captured EVPs on this investigation. They captured the following EVP's and unexplained noises on DVR's and microcassette recorder: In the attic they captured 2 unexplained knocks, 2 unexplained breaths, an unexplained noise, and an unexplained breath and knock. In the basement they captured these EVPs: unexplained noise, unexplained female whisper, unexplained knocking and a yell, a whisper saying, "Hey", then a click, and lastly another whisper.

They also captured several EVPs in the Bride's Room and the Children's Room. They captured a whisper in the Bride's Room. In the Children's Room they captured a female voice saying, "Justin", an unexplained noise, a nock, a loud bang, someone whispering, "Brad", a whisper and a low moan, a loud click, and an unexplained noise that sounded like something dropped and hit the floor, but no one was in the house at the time.

In the Master Bedroom BDPS captured the following EVPs: an unexplained voice, scratching, a breath and a whisper simultaneously, then a voice and lastly a female voice saying, "Right". In the Slave House they captured EVPs of random noises and footsteps that could not be explained away.

BDPS have concluded that the Major Graham Mansion has very high paranormal activity in the forms of EVP's, interesting photographic orbs, unexplained dark mass, audio and video evidence which showed an unexplained apparition, and unexplained formation of lights or orbs and personal experiences that helped us to determine our conclusion.

But is it haunted? In 2007, the Virginia Paranormal Society (VPS) began performing formal investigations at the mansion.

Over the course of three years, several paranormal groups have assisted VPS and collected hundreds of EVPs (i.e., electronic voice phenomena), and experienced paranormal contact at the mansion. VPS reports that many of its members have communicated with the dominant spirits of Martha Peirce Graham, Squire David Graham, and "Clara" a Civil War orphan who secretly lived (and died!) at the mansion. In addition, they have a collection of ghost stories and photos from the community as well as anecdotal reports from guest clairvoyants. What do you think?

Case 023 Major Graham Mansion 6/26/10

Case 023 Major Graham Mansion 6/26/10 unexplained orbs

Case 023 Major Graham Mansion 6/26/10

Chapter 6
Historical Molly Tynes Home / Stiltner Home

History

Black Diamond Paranormal Society had the honor of investigating the historical "Rocky Dell," in Tazewell County VA, home of local Civil War heroin Molly Tynes.

Rocky Dell has an amazingly rich history surrounding the time period of the Civil War. The home was constructed in 1860 and immediately occupied by Samuel and Frances Tynes. Their son Achilles J. Tynes was away during the early 60's due to his officer status (Captain) in the CSA Army. Their daughter Mary Elizabeth (aka "Molly") was away at Hollins College in Botetourt County, VA. Samuel's wife Frances was elderly and ill. Samuel himself was getting up there in age and seriously needed an extra hand on the farm. So, Molly rose to the call and came back home to take care of her mother and father. However, nobody knew that a simple return home would change the pages of history and make her name live on in infamy.

On July of 1863, Colonial J.T. Toland of the 34th Ohio Infantry took command of a little more than 1,000 Federal soldiers, mobilized his unit and trekked from Huntington, WV to Jeffersonville, VA (current day Tazewell). His orders were that of a 'scorched earth' scenario from Jeffersonville to Wytheville to Saltville. Their main targets were the Confederate salt mines at Saltville (Smyth County), destroy the lead mines in Wythe County, and annihilate the Virginia & Tennessee Railroad lines at Wytheville. With any of the 3 mission objectives complete, the Confederacy would have taken such a blow that the war would have almost immediately came to a standstill. Without this geographically important bullet and munitions depot, the Rebels didn't stand a chance. This is where the "Ms. Molly" comes into the story.

After Colonial Toland set up camp in Ben Bolt (Jeffersonville) next to the Tynes' farm, the Tynes' family learned the details of the Federal Army's plans for the mass mobilization that had invaded the area. With the knowledge of what was about to unfold, Molly and her father decided that the impending invasion must be stopped at all costs. Their only hope was Molly herself and her trusted horse 'Fashion.' So, on the night of July 17, 1863, Molly and Fashion set forth on the most important journey of their lives.

Molly used the veil of the night to make her escape from the farm, turning in the direction of Burkes Garden and riding 40 miles through the mountainous wilderness to Wytheville. During her ride she channeled Paul Revere as she valiantly screamed through the night her warning that 'The Yankees are coming.'

According to oral tradition, upon receiving Molly's

message, locals immediately went to arms, banding together to form last minute militias and calling for Confederate reinforcements to defend the target areas.

Due to Molly's heroism, swift action and bravery, countless Confederate civilians were spared the destruction of their homes, farms and even their lives. Not only did she save the locals from being taken off guard by Toland's Army, she saved the railroad, salt mines and lead mines. Also due to Molly's advance notice, the people of Wytheville were prepared enough to set up sniping positions within their homes and from rooftops. When the Federal Army finally made its way to Tazewell Street, Colonial Toland was immediately shot and killed by the forewarned townspeople. This left his unit with no leader, thus the surviving members of his detachment were forced to retreat and escaped through the adjacent woods.

After Molly's wild ride, she was regarded as a local hero. However, since the time period still dictated that this was a 'man's world' little was written about Molly during the time. Most of what has been documented is just written recreations of the oral accounts and local legends of that fateful night.

While some details are unclear and others contested, the following are generally accepted amongst scholars and historical researchers to be the undeniable facts surrounding the incident in which Molly is infamous for:

- July 17th, 1863 – Either Molly herself or her father Samuel overheard the local Federal Troops' plans to invade Wytheville and Saltville.
- Molly did in fact ride to Wytheville.
- The townspeople of Wytheville were warned prior to the invasion due to written records from a local CSA detachment that states such.
- The home that B.D.P.S. investigated is the one and same known as 'Rocky Dell' (aka the Tynes farm).

No matter what the minor details were added or left out, the undeniable fact is Molly Tynes is a remarkable woman for her heroism and bravery. No history report or summary can sum it up better than a song written about this historic event.

Reports & Claims:

There have been reports of unexplained disembodied voices, apparitions, shadows, mists, lights, orbs.

Investigation

On November 13, 2010 the BDPS team investigated the Historical Molly Tynes Home located in Tazewell, Virginia. The investigators on this case was Rodney Shortridge, Aaron Shortridge, Mike Brown, Matt O'Quin, Clayton Trout, Dr. Shari Stacy Dave Horn, Michele Crigger and (Guest) Jeff Vance.

Permission to investigate this property was granted by Mr. Roger Stiltner.

BDPS decided because of the size of the home that each team would investigate separate areas of the property and structures simultaneously while one team would watch the camera monitors at base camp within the home. They began their investigation around 6:00 p.m. with a walking tour of the house that was given by Mr. Stiltner. They began their set up around 7:00 p.m., then proceeded to the investigation soon after dividing into teams. Team 1 consisted of Rodney, Clayton Trout and Dr. Shari Stacy. Team 2 consisted of Mike Brown, Matt O'Quin and their newest member Michele Crigger. Team 3 consisted of Aaron Shortridge, Dave Horn and (Guest) Jeff Vance. Each team was placed in certain locations to investigate the home and property, with one team investigating the outside grounds near a huge tree that is rumored to be a place where a Union soldier was hanged, while one team monitored their cameras back at base and another team investigated the inside of the home. Each team worked on a rotation changing their location about every 2 hours. BDPS finished their investigation around 3:00 a.m. the following morning.

Equipment used during this investigation is as follows: 6 DVR's (Digital Voice Recorders, 1 microcassette recorder, 4 zero lux low lever IR (infra-red) cameras, 1 Panasonic handheld camcorder, 1 Sony handheld camcorder, 2 Kodak digital cameras, 0 Nikon camera, 1 Fuji digital camera, 1 Canon digital camera, 2

Samsung digital cameras, 0 motion diction IR (infra-red) Field video/camera, 2 K2 meters, 2) EMF (Electro Magnetic Field) meter, 2 laser thermometers, 1 Frank's Box, 1 Plasma Ball and 1 power mic.

BDPS placed 1 DVR in each of the areas of the property with reports or claims of paranormal activity. This included the upstairs bedroom, downstairs bedroom, living room, dining room, Molly's bedroom and the main entrance way. The IR Cameras were also placed in areas of reported activity. 1 IR camera was placed in the main entrance way to cover the stairs and the entrance way. 1 was placed in the upstairs bedroom. 1 was placed in Molly's bedroom and 1 was placed in the living room. 1 Panasonic handheld camcorder was placed in the downstairs bedroom and 1 Sony handheld camcorder was carried around by me during the investigation. 1 microcassette recorder was carried by each team during the investigation. Also, each team carried along with them during their investigations one of the following: K2 meter, EMF meter or laser thermometer.

Personal Experiences:

While investigating the upstairs bedroom along with Clayton Trout and Dr. Shari Stacy, Rodney felt something brush throw his hair. Clayton and Rodney checked the area in which they were standing to check for spider webs, cobwebs, any bugs that may have fallen into his hair and they could not find anything to explain the occurrence.

Later that night while watching the monitors with Clayton and Shari, Rodney stated having this enormous feeling of doing harm and violence to Clayton, Shari and to all his team mates to the point it was causing him so much discomfort and the feeling of losing control that he immediately left the house and went to his truck to clear his head and try to figure out what was happening. He couldn't understand why would he have the thoughts to harm these people that were his friends that meant the world to him? Rodney loves fellow investigators like family, however the images in his head of doing unspeakable harm to them was so strong that it was making him begin to question his own judgment. After about 40 minutes his head was clearer but he still had this sense of something trying to control his thoughts.

Rodney rejoined the investigation and within the hour the feelings of rage ran through his mind like all the things throughout his life that had upset him came back in a flood of emotions and anger. Once again, he left the investigation to go get away from the house to clear his thoughts. He began to realize that something in the house was trying to influence his thoughts to the point of causing him pain. After about an hour Rodney regained composure and made the decision that it would be best if he did not stay in the house for a long period of time for the safety of the team and himself.

For three days following the investigation he felt this rage and anger towards everyone. He tried to seclude himself from the people that were around him for fear of losing control to the rage that was building inside him. But as quickly as the rage and the evil thoughts that ran through his mind seemed to vanish just as quickly as they came. He doesn't have an explanation for this. He is unsure as to whether it was a demon, evil spirit, or something else? BDPS might not ever know but speaking with the team about this Rodney found out that three others on the team seemed to have experiences of their own.

One member was deeply depressed after the investigation for three days, another member had an experience at their home when they returned from this investigation and another member said their personality seemed changed to the point that their partner even noticed odd things about them and it lasted for three days. This investigation added more questions than answers because it affected so many of the BDPS team and Rodney in ways that is almost impossible to put into words.

Evidence and Conclusion

BDPS captured photographic evidence of unexplained orbs and unexplained lights. They captured video evidence as well consisting of an unexplained light on the bed in the upstairs room, along with an object that hovers near Dr. Stacy's head.

BDPS captured several EVPs. They heard the following EVP's and unexplained noises on our DVR's and microcassette recorder: In the dining room they captured an unexplained noise, a voice saying, "Go", and an unexplained moan an unexplained whisper saying, "That's _____". Then in the master bedroom upstairs they caught these EVPs, a whisper, an unexplained knock and whisper saying, "Guess who?", whistling, an unexplained noise, a female voice whispering, "Hannah ----- Hannah", from Frank's box a voice saying, "Turkey", a female humming, unexplained footsteps and a male voice whispering, "No" and an unexplained noise after the EVP.

And EVPs captured in Molly's bedroom were as follows: a male voice whispering, "Oh my God ----- Oh my God", and a child's voice saying, "Daddy".

BDPS have concluded that the Historical Molly Tynes Home has paranormal activity in the form of EVP's, unexplained photographic orbs, unexplained lights, audio and video evidence which showed an unexplained white mass, and unexplained formation of lights or orbs and personal experiences.

Case 028 Molly Tynes Home 11/13/10

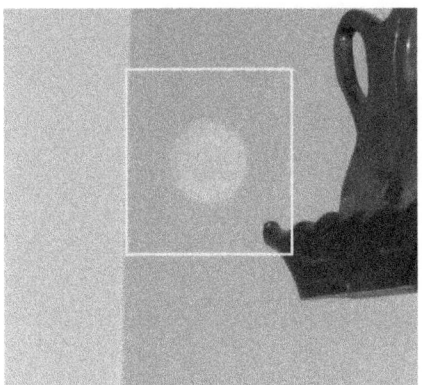

Case 028 Molly Tynes Home 11/13/10 unexplained orbs

Chapter 7
Undisclosed Location (Anonymous Clients)

Reports and Claims

Client claims that due to high amounts of unexplained whispers in the child's bedroom, the child is unable to sleep in this bedroom. The clients have seen a black shadow pass through the kitchen area. There are claims of seeing a child called "Little Jacob" in the living room, dining room and the hallway of the home.

Investigation

On July 27, 2012 the BDPS team investigated an undisclosed location. The client requested to be anonymous due to the nature of this case. The investigators on this case was Rodney Shortridge, Jason Kwun, Matt O'Quin, Michele Crigger and Robyn Dalton.

BDPS decided because of the size of the home they would conduct the investigation with two teams. Rodney would watch the monitors and be a float to help out each team during the investigation while the other teams conducted the investigation throughout the home. They began the investigation around 7:00

p.m. The clients gave a walking tour of the home to BDPS historian Dave Horn while interviewing for the pre-investigating a few weeks prior to the investigation, the clients gave BDPS a quick walk through of the home to update them on any new claims.

They began their set up around 7:30 p.m. then proceeded to their investigation after dividing up into two teams. Team one was Jason and Michele, team two which consisted of Matt and Robyn. Rodney watched the monitor and experimented with taking long exposed time photos throughout the investigation while each time was investigating. BDPS worked on a rotation changing their location about every 2 hours. They finished the investigation around 3:00 a.m. the following morning.

The equipment used during this investigation is as follows: 4 DVR's (Digital Voice Recorders, 4) zero lux low lever IR (infra-red) cameras, 1 Sony handheld camcorder, 2 Kodak digital cameras, 1 Canon digital camera, 0 Motion diction IR (infra-red) field video/camera, 1 K2 meters, 1 EMF (Electro Magnetic Field) meter, and 1 laser thermometers.

BDPS placed 1 DVR in each of the areas of the home with reports or claims of paranormal activity, which included the child's bedroom, dining room, hallway and the living room. 1 IR camera was placed in the daughter's room, 1 IR camera was placed in the dining room, 1 IR camera was placed in the hallway, and 1 IR camera was placed in the living room. All locations for the IR cameras were placed for maximum view for areas were the paranormal activity claims were the strongest. Also, BDPS carried along with us during the investigation one of the following: K2 meter, EMF (Electro Magnetic Field) meter, laser thermometer and a Sony handheld camcorder.

Personal Experiences

Rodney and Robyn investigated the house on Thursday night and Friday Morning July 26/27 from about 10:45 p.m.-12:00 a.m. Rodney's personal experiences are as follows: before the investigation began when the team did a walk through with the client a bell made a sound that sounded very much like one on a bicycle. The client said he did not have one in the house. It is possible that this bell was from someone riding a bicycle outside on the sidewalk. This piece of evidence cannot be neither debunked nor confirmed.

While Rodney and Robyn were conducting EVP sessions in the child's room Rodney was sitting against the wall asking questions. After approximately 15-25 minutes into the session they took a break and during that break Rodney audibly heard someone whisper, "What" near Rodney's right ear. Robyn heard something but could not make it out from where she was sitting. Upon hearing this Rodney became a bit unsettled. This was the first time he had ever heard an audible voice with his own ear during an investigation. Rodney cannot explain where this voice came from. In Rodney's opinion this could be a paranormal anomaly.

When Rodney later came back into the house with me and

Robyn he was taking pictures of us in the child's room. He had a flashlight on the floor in front of his legs beside their toy piano. During his shooting a flash of light came from the toy piano after some explicit questions coming from Rodney. This flash could be attributed to the laser finder on the camera, but Rodney cannot say for certain.

Other than that, no other major experiences took place however various sounds, smells, feelings, and senses came from the child's room and the adjacent area just outside the room in the hallway. All sounds that could not be explained came from this area.

At 10:19 p.m. Jason and Michele experienced unexplained scents in the kitchen that they were unable to trace to any sources within the kitchen area. Jason and Michele also experienced unexplained knocking noises from the front door of the home with no one being present at the main entrance; this was collaborated by Rodney that had the van parked by the entrance way and he reported not seeing anyone at the outside of the door at any of the times of the unexplained knocking was occurring. Jason and Michele also experienced unexplained cold chills walking into the child's bedroom.

While Rodney was taking photos throughout the home an unexplained blue light was captured on a still shot camera set at a 15 second exposure time with no flash on five different photos while Matt and Robyn were in the child's bedroom investigating.

Jason and Rodney were in the hallway trying to figure out

where the cold spots he and Michele had experienced might have originated. While investigating the air vents, they both heard a male voice say, "What". The unexplained voice was heard between Jason and Rodney. They were only approximately 3 feet apart when they heard this voice. Jason and Rodney were the only two males in the home at the time.

Evidence and Conclusion

BDPS captured photographic evidence in the form of an unexplained blue light captured on a still shot camera set at a 15 second exposure time with no flash on five different photos. They also captured video evidence of two different unexplained objects in the child's bedroom, at the same time while Jason and Michele were investigating the bedroom; a blurred object was seen moving towards and around Michele's back and an unexplained flash of light over Michele's head.

BDPS also captured several EVPs and unexplained noises on their DVR's and microcassette recorder. In the child's room they captured an unexplained voice saying, "Yes", and an unexplained whisper saying, "What". In the dining room and kitchen area they caught a female voice saying, "Love me", a female voice saying, "Your dead", unexplained footsteps, a female voice say, "Rodney, (*Breath*) Rodney, (*Breath*) Rodney".

In the hallway BDPS captured the following EVPs: of a growl and a voice say, "Yes".

In the living room they captured a female sigh/moan, an undistinguishable female voice, an unexplained knock/popping noise, a low undistinguishable whisper and a male voice say, "Yes".

BDPS have concluded that the home has moderate paranormal activity. They were able to capture a few EVP's, video and photographic evidence which helped us to make this determination. BDPS feels that this may be moderate intelligent energy. They were able to obtain enough evidence to back most of the claims of the client.

Chapter 8
Ramsey School Building

History

Ramsey School in Bluefield West Virginia has at least one claim to fame. Many years ago, it was featured in "Ripley's Believe It or Not" because it has entrances on seven different levels. The school was built at the corner of two streets, each of which is quite steep. So, the two roads wrap around it in an ever-increasing incline, it is truly beloved in its neighborhood.

With classes closing in 1987, it has recently been brought back to life by developer, Tony Szabo, from Seattle.

Reports and Claims

The client says he hasn't had any paranormal experiences within the building but has been told of stories of paranormal activity by patrons and people within the community of unexplained sounds and unexplained voices within the building.

Investigation

On April 8, 2013 the BDPS team investigated the Ramsey

School Building in Bluefield West Virginia. Investigators for this case was Rodney Shortridge, Michele Crigger, Robyn Dalton, Aaron Shortridge, Scott Osmundson, Olivia Compton and Jeff Dalton BDPS obtained permission to investigate the school by owner Mr. Tony Szabo. It was decided because of the size of the building BDPS would conduct the investigation with three teams. Rodney would investigate alone and later throughout the night he would float to work with each team.

BDPS began the investigation around 7:00 p.m. A walking tour of the building was given by the client a few weeks prior to the investigation to Dave Horn, Michele Crigger, Aaron Shortridge and Rodney Shortridge while interviewing for the pre-investigating. The evening of the investigation the client gave BDPS a walkthrough of the building to update us on any new claims.

BDPS began their set up at approximately 7:30 p.m. They then proceeded to conduct the investigation after dividing into three teams. Team one was Robyn and Jeff, team two consisted of Michele and BDPS's new trainee Olivia and team three consisted of Aaron and Scott. Rodney investigated alone and experimented with taking long exposed time photos while each team investigated. BDPS worked on a rotation changing locations about every 2 hours. They concluded the investigation at approximately 3:00 a.m. the following morning.

Equipment used during the investigation as follows: 4 DVR's (Digital Voice Recorders), 0 Zero Lux low lever IR (infra-red) cameras, 1 Sony handheld camcorder, 2 Kodak digital cameras, 1 Canon digital camera, 0 Motion diction IR (infra-red) field video/camera, 1 K2 meters, 1 EMF (Electro Magnetic Field) meter, 1) laser thermometers.

BDPS placed 1 DVR in each of the areas of the building with reports or claims of paranormal activity, which included the second-floor bar. Each team carried on their person a digital recorder to record any experiences or EVP's they encountered during the investigation. Due to the size of the building and four floors to cover they decided it would be best for each team to carry a DVR. Also, due to the complexity of the building such as size and distances, to cover within the building it was decided that IR Camera's would be ineffective. However, they did use the Sony handheld camera along with digital cameras to film during the investigation. They also carried with them during the investigation one of the following: K2 Meter, EMF (Electro Magnetic Field) meter, and laser thermometer.

Personal Experiences

Olivia Compton had several unforgettable personal experiences at the Ramsey School building investigation in Bluefield, West Virginia.

Michele and Olivia began their investigation in the auditorium. They both experienced chills and felling sick. Olivia felt cold chills—one on her right side as they were sitting there trying to communication with the spirits. She held out her hand and asked if whoever was there could they touch her. That's when she felt her entire arm go completely cold. Michele took pictures the entire night. They later heard a loud bang that came from the corner of the auditorium. The source of the sound cannot be explained. Throughout the night they both experienced cold chills and creepy feelings. However, it was nothing compared to the feelings they felt on the fourth floor.

As Michele and Olivia walked up the stairs Olivia told Michele that she had a "bad vibe" about that floor. That's when they both began having difficulty breathing. Olivia mentioned this to Michele, and she said that she was having difficulty breathing as well. They ventured into one of the classrooms and saw a dead black bird. The odd thing was, that it was only two feet away from the toy guitar that they placed there earlier; they found it hard to believe that they had missed that earlier. The atmosphere began getting thicker which made it more uncomfortable for them.

As the two walked out to the stairwell again, Olivia told Michele that she felt like they shouldn't go up to the old band room. There was no explanation; it was just a gut feeling. But Michele insisted they go up there for at least a few minutes. That's when things got "real". Their breathing patterns became so abnormal that it was affecting their health. Michele became unstable and began to sway. Olivia began having lung spasms and felt pressure on her chest.

Michele moved toward the window and Olivia joined her to

try and get some fresh air. A few seconds later Olivia told Michele that it wasn't working and that we should leave. As soon as Olivia turned around, Michele stated that her back was on fire! Olivia looked at Michele's back and found that she had been scratched in three places. Olivia photographed pictures of the scratches and showed Michele, that's when Michele almost fainted. Olivia managed to get Michele back down the stairs and met up with Aaron and Scott; they took over helping Michele back down to the main lobby.

Evidence and Conclusion

BDPS captured photographic evidence on this investigation in the form of unexplained blue light streak captured on a still shot camera. However, they did not capture any video evidence. They did get K2 hits but BDPS determined that it was old wiring. Aaron and Scott found anomalies high electromagnetic K-2 readings on the second-floor balcony which was determined to be from the wiring, we suggest that the owner have an electrician to check the wiring due to such high readings.

EVPs were captured. EVP's and unexplained noises on our DVR's and microcassette recorder is as follows: on the 2nd floor Bar Room on the Bar they captured an unexplained female voice saying something undistinguishable after Michele speaks. The recorders on Aaron Shortridge & Scott Osmundson captured 2 unexplained whispers saying, "Yeah, Yeah" while Scott and Aaron were talking, an unexplained child's voice, an unexplained male whisper saying, "Cocky, Cocky" while Scott was speaking, an unexplained voice saying, "Was" and an unexplained knock.

Michele Crigger & Olivia Compton captured these EVPs; an unexplained noise, an unexplained faint moan (and Olivia heard it audibly), an unexplained female voice whispering, "Get Back Up", and an unexplained moan while Olivia was talking. Rodney Shortridge captured these EVPs; an unexplained loud giggle and an unexplained voice saying, "Don't Stop".

BDPS have concluded that the building seems to have a significant amount of paranormal activity. They were able to capture a few EVP's and photographic evidence. They feel that their findings are too inconclusive and more research and investigation over a longer period of time may help with the understanding of the evidence they collected.

Case 038 Ramsey Building Bluefield WV 4/8/13

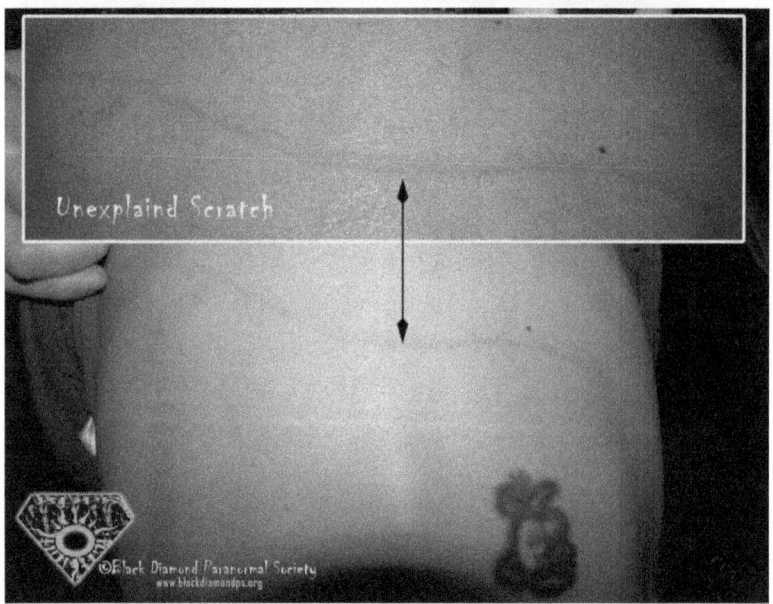

Case 038 Ramsey Building Bluefield WV 4/8/13 unexplained scratches on Michele Crigger

Chapter 9
Mayhew Home

History

BDPS was unable to find any historical information on the home.

Reports and Claims

There have been reports of glass sliding across the counter top, dishes breaking, a dark entity seen in the first child's bedroom, sounds of unexplained foots steps walking across the floor, unexplained voices and in the grandfathers bedroom a lady dressed in white has been seen.

Investigation

On August 16, 2014 the BDPS team investigated the Mayhew Home located in Morristown TN. The investigators on this case were Rodney Shortridge, Matt O'Quin, Michele Crigger, Robyn Dalton, Aaron Shortridge, Olivia Compton, David Belcher and Jeff Dalton.

BDPS decided because of the size of the home that they

would have one team investigating inside while one team watched the camera monitor and then each team would wait until their turn for rotation. They began the investigation at approximately 6:00 p.m. with a walking tour of the home that was given by the renter of the home. They began their set up around 7:00 p.m. They then proceeded to their investigation. Soon after they divided into teams. Team 1 consisted of Rodney and Michele, Team 2 consisted of Robyn and Matt, Team 3 consisted of Jeff and David, and Team 4 consisted of Olivia and Aaron. Each team worked on a rotation changing their location about every 1 ½ hour. They concluded their investigation at approximately 3:00 a.m. the following morning.

Equipment used on this investigation were as follows: 4 DVR's (Digital Voice Recorders), 4 Zero Lux low lever IR (infrared) cameras, 1 Sony handheld camcorder, 3 digital cameras, 1 Canon digital camera, 2 K2 meters, 1 EMF (Electro Magnetic Field) meter and 1 laser thermometers. They placed 1 DVR (Digital Voice Recorder) in each of the areas of the home with reports or claims of paranormal activity; including the kitchen, first children's room, second children's room and the grandfather's bedroom. 1 IR camera was placed in the kitchen, 1 was placed in the in the hallway, 1 was placed in the first children's bedroom and 1 was placed in the second children's bedroom. 1 Sony handheld camcorder was carried around by Rodney. Also, each team carried along with them during their investigations one of the following: DVR, K2 meter or EMF (Electro Magnetic Field) meter or laser thermometer.

Personal Experiences

As Jeff and David began their investigation in the kitchen of the home, a shelf in the cabinet in the corner collapsed and all the contents fell to the floor. They determined the possible reason for the collapsed shelf was due to the weight of the contents on the shelf. The shelf collapsing was not due to paranormal activity.

Evidence and Conclusion

There was no photographic evidence captured and no video evidence captured on this investigation. However, there were several EVPs captured on this investigation. They heard the following EVP's and unexplained noises on their DVR's and microcassette recorder. In the first child's bedroom they caught the following EVPs: an unexplained female voice saying, "grace here", an unexplained glass clanking, an unexplained low female voice saying "Mommy", an unexplained male voice saying, "Rodney did it", an unexplained noise (Robyn and Matt heard this audibly), an unexplained noise for a second time (Robyn heard this audibly).

In the second children's bedroom these EVPs were captured, two different unexplained moaning noises at the same time, an unexplained female voice whispering, "Nothing" while Robyn was speaking, an unexplained undistinguishable female voice before Robyn spoke, an unexplained low whisper saying,

"Help" with a K2 hit and an unexplained low moan.

In the grandfather's bedroom BDPS caught the following EVPs: an unexplained voice saying, "Huh", and female voice saying, "That's it", an unexplained female moaning, an unexplained undistinguishable voice, a low whispering, "Give me a hug", a male voice saying, "Do it on your own", a male voice saying, "Hey girls", a male voice saying, "Rodney", a male voice saying, "Shit", a smacking sound, a voice saying, "You're an ass", whispers saying "House" 4 different times while Michele and Olivia were speaking about the house, someone whispering, "Get a brain", and someone whispering, "House" at the same time Rodney is saying house, and whispering or chanting.

These EVPs were captured in the kitchen: a breathe on two different occasion, a female voice saying, "It's berries" with a giggle, glass clanking or spoon in coffee cup sound, a hissing sound, a low whisper, low whispering of someone saying, "Come back" and a voice saying, "Berries".

BDPS concluded that the client's home has moderate paranormal activity in the forms of EVP's, unexplained K-2 hits.

Case 042 Susan Mayhew Home Morristown TN 8/16/14

Chapter 10
Patton Crosswhite Post 6975 VFW

History

The Patton Crosswhite Post 6975 VFW was charted in 1946 and received the building from Southern Railroad in 1951. The building has been a canteen and a hospital for World War I veterans. Before Patton Crosswhite the VFW was known as Rebel Retreat. They were located in Virginia and moved to Tennessee due to alcohol being outlawed.

There are several different areas of the building including a Women Auxiliary Room where the women held their meetings and worked on the VFW scrapbooks. A meeting room upstairs that now contains mostly photographs of the post's past history along with photos of celebrities, car shows, dances, fundraisers and of Senator Richard Nixon who visited Bristol TN in 1949 and the VFW Honor Guard procession during the Senators visit. Also, upstairs was a designated room for very distinguished members called the Royal Order of the Cooties. The building has several hidden passages used to hide gambling machines that were illegal at that time. Also, hidden in the walls and passages, they have found many artifacts and some that have not been identified to date.

On the main floor is the lounge and dining room areas which have many military artifacts such as the ship's wheel of the CSS Merrimac. This ship's wheel was originally on the USS Virginia it was captured and turned into an Iron Clad Ship the CSS Merrimac. In the lounge room is a display case with a Confederate Soldier's uniform. The uniform belonged to General Howell who in fact was not a General but a Corporal in the Confederate Army. General Howell enlisted in the Civil War as a Confederate Soldier. He was from Southeastern VA. General Howell died in the 1940's at the age of 105. At the time of his death there were only 4 remaining surviving Confederate Soldiers still alive. Also, at that time of his death he was the last President of the UCV (United Confederate Veterans Association of America). When General Howell died it gave birth to the Sons of Confederacy. General Howell had also been President of Virginia Intermont College. General Howell spoke of the Civil War in a recording that can be heard today on YouTube called "Confederate "General" Julius Howell Recalls the 1860's" at: https://youtu.be/uHDfC-z9YaE

The Grand Ball Room is also located on the main floor which was added in the late 1950's. The room has been used for many special events and for entertainment. However, tragedy did occur in the 1950's or 60's when an unknown lady was killed by a stabbing and again in 1989 when Donna Joyner was knifed down by her husband.

Two very important men that helped shape and build the VFW to what it is today are Guy Richardson also known as Mr. VFW Mr. Richardson who later became the Mayor of Bristol TN, and Olan Unpower. These men are known as the corner stone to the VFW.

Reports and Claims

There have been two murders that have been confirmed at this location along with two past employees dyeing months after leaving their jobs. The murder of Donna Joyner occurred on the ballroom floor at a dance. She was murdered by her husband in 1989. Another murder of an unnamed young lady took place during the 1950's or 1960's. Each murder was a grizzly knife attack that left two women dead with the post and community in shock.

There have been multiple paranormal reports and claims at the post such as, sounds of moving metal chairs when no one was in the room, feelings of being led to find artifacts hidden within the walls, claims of two different female disembodied voices, one personal experience while the Air Force song was playing on the juke box, there were sightings of Confederate Soldiers in full gear and a dark shadow. There were also, claims of an evil looking woman's face. These sightings and experiences caused extreme emotional feelings of sadness and anxiety. Sounds of the bell located in the lounge area being rung with no one in the room, doors shutting on their own, and in the bathroom located in the lounge area people have had feelings of being extremely uncomfortable, unexplained sightings of a male standing on the landing have occurred. There have also been reports of unexplained scent of something rotten following people around even after the room had been cleaned. There have been sightings of General Howell upstairs, unexplained shadows around the exit sign and doorway, and uneasy feelings located at the hot water heater room.

Investigation

On March 15, 2015 the BDPS team investigated Patton Crosswhite Post 6975 VFW located in Bristol, Tennessee. Investigators on this case was Rodney Shortridge, Michele Crigger, Robyn Dalton, Jeff Dalton, David Belcher and Pat Belcher.

BDPS decided because of the size of the building that each team would investigate separate areas of the property simultaneously while one team would watch the camera monitors at base camp within the building. They began the investigation at approximately 8:00 p.m. with a walking tour of the post that was given by Tommy Porter. They began set up around 9:00 p.m. They then proceeded to their investigation soon after dividing into teams. Team 1 consisted of Michele Crigger and Pat Belcher, Team 2 consisted of Robyn Dalton and David Belcher and Rodney watched the camera monitors. They were assisted throughout the night during the investigation by Tommy Porter, Donna Tomblin and Mrs. Porter. Each team was placed to investigate different locations of the building, with team 1 investigating the second floor and surrounding rooms, and team 2 investigating the bar and lounge area on the first floor while Rodney monitored the cameras back at base. Each team worked on a rotation changing their location about every 2 hours. The investigation concluded at around 4:00 a.m. the following morning.

Equipment used during the investigation: 5 DVR's (Digital Voice Recorders), 6 IR (infra-red) cameras, 2 Kodak digital cameras, 1 Fuji digital camera, 1 Canon digital camera, 2 Samsung digital cameras, 2 K2 meters, 1 EMF (Electro Magnetic Field) meter, 1 laser thermometers.

BDPS placed 1 DVR in each of the areas of the building with reports or claims of paranormal activity; including the bar, lounge, ballroom and the women's auxiliary room. Each team took turns carrying and using a DVR for live EVP sessions. 1 IR camera was placed in the lounge, 2 were placed in the ballroom, 2 were placed in the bar 1 was placed in the in the hallway of our base. Also, each team carried along with them during their investigations one of the following: K2 Meter, EMF meter or laser thermometer.

Weather Readings

At 6:46 p.m. Sunny 67, Due point 30%, Humidity 28%, N

x NW winds 13, Bar Pressure 30.15

Personal Experiences

At 10:55 p.m. while watching the camera monitors Jeff and Rodney heard a noise like a gravel had been tossed and hit the main entrance door and floor behind them, Jeff turned on the lights in the room and they both investigated to try and find what had made the noise and to try and find the gravel or whatever the object was that they heard, but after both of them looked around on the floor and behind all the furniture we could not find any object to explain what they had heard.

Evidence and Conclusion

There was no photographic evidence nor video evidence during this investigation. There were only a few EVPs. BDPS captured the following EVP's and unexplained noises on our DVR's and microcassette recorder: in the Grand Ball Room a female voice saying, "It's fun", a female voice saying, "Um get the vultures", a male voice saying, "Oh my God...I'm God" and an older female voice that is undistinguishable.

BDPS came to the conclusion that the Patton Crosswhite Post 6975 VFW has very low paranormal activity. They determined this from their findings in the forms of EVP's and personal experiences.

Case 043 VFW Post 6975 Bristol TN 3/15/15

Case 043 VFW Post 6975 Bristol TN 3/15/15
In the lounge room is a display case with a Confederate soldier's uniform. The uniform belonged to General Howell, who in face was not a General but a Corporal in the Confederate Army. General Howell enlisted in the Civil War as a Confederate Soldier. He was from Southeastern VA. General Howell died in the 1940's at the age of 105.

Chapter 11
Nickerson Snead House Museum

History

Dr. Nickerson & Betsy Snead built this beautiful Antebellum home circa 1835, however the original log portion of this historical haunted Nickerson Snead House was built in the 1700s by Francis Kincannon. This magnificent home was used as a Civil War field hospital and the cellar was used as a temporary morgue. After Nickerson and Betsy Snead passed away the property was sold to the Masons who owned the Antebellum from the late 1800s until the late 1980s. In 2004 it was purchased by Ricky and Ronda Caudill, who currently own it.

The Nickerson Snead House is open to the public to enjoy a variety of events including historical haunted tours, craft festivals, murder mystery dinners, ladies' Victorian high tea, living history, overnight paranormal investigations, and is transformed into a haunted house attraction for 6 weeks every fall.

Reports and Claims

There have been reports of shadow figures, a woman in blue, touching, laughing, talking, things being moved, music, walking sounds, seeing things being moved, bells ringing, apparitions, feelings of being watched and phantom smells all throughout the house.

Investigation

On March 19, 2016 the BDPS team investigated the Nickerson Snead House Museum located in Glade Spring VA. Investigators on this case were as follows: Rodney Shortridge, Robyn Dalton, Jeff Dalton and Scott Osmundson. Trainees: Josh and Breonna Fuller, Nate Wheeler and Will Rash.

They were asked by Ronda Caudill to investigate this location. They decided because of the size of the home that they would have one team investigating inside while one team watched the camera monitor and then each team would wait until their turn for rotation. They began the investigation around 7:00 p.m. They began their our set up around 7:00 p.m. and then proceeded to the investigation. Soon after they divided into teams. Team 1 consisted of Robyn Dalton and Breonna Fuller, Team 2 consisted of Scott Osmundson and Nate Wheeler, Team 3 consisted of Jeff Dalton and Will Rash, and Team 4 consisted of Rodney Shortridge and Josh Fuller. Each team worked on a rotation changing their location about every 1 ½ hour. They concluded their investigation around 3:00 a.m. the following morning.

Equipment used during this investigation were as follows: 6 DVR's (Digital Voice Recorders), 8 Zero Lux low lever IR (infra-red) cameras, 2 Digital cameras, 1 Canon digital camera, 2 K2 meters, 1 EMF (Electro Magnetic Field) meter, and 1 laser thermometer.

They placed 1 DVR in each of the areas of the home with reports or claims of paranormal activity; including the hallway by the kitchen, basement, entryway, upstairs hallway, white bedroom and one that was carried by each team during their investigation. 1 IR camera was placed in the kitchen, 1 was placed in the in the basement, 1 was placed in the downstairs hallway, 1 was placed at the front stairs, 1 was placed in the parlor room, 1 was placed in the red room, 1 was placed at the upper hallway and 1 was placed in the white room. Also, each team carried along with them during their investigations one of the following: DVR, K2 meter, EMF meter or laser thermometer.

Weather Readings

Local weather at the time of the investigation: 45 degrees, cloudy pressure: 29.9, dew point:41, visibility: 9 miles, wind; N x NE 7miles, 85% humidity and chance of snow.

Each room was swept with K-2 and laser thermometer: Basement 44 degrees high EMF readings throughout entire basement due to exposed wiring, Red Room 53 degrees no EMF readings, dinning room 55 – 60 degrees no EMF readings, stairway by entry 52 – 53 degrees light switch K-2 hit, Upstairs Hall 49 degrees moderate K-2 hit on middle window, pink room 51 – 53 degrees K-2 hit on light switch, green room 52-53 degrees no K-2 hits, front entryway 48-50 degrees K-2 hits wall with switches lights at doorway near glass window, parlor room 48-49 degrees K-2 hits poles at window, hallway between entryway 49-53 degrees K-2 hits light switch at stairs exit sign and outlets, kitchen 51-57 degrees K-2 hits center with table, floor and wall at the first doorway, stove.

Personal Experiences

Scott Osmundson and Nate Wheeler's Personal Experiences: Tapping on glass in response to questions in parlor room. Also, Scott thought he heard breathing while live recording also in the parlor room and he smelled the scent of perfume in the parlor room.

Rodney was outside in the parking area around 2:00 a.m. While two teams where coming out of the house and walking down the walkway Rodney noticed a glowing orange light in the middle of the second-floor window that looked like a large candle or an old lantern. The light moved across the upper staircase and down the steps that leads to the front door as if someone were carrying the light down the steps. Then it looked like the light moved back and forth as someone was walking down the steps with the light. Rodney rushed up to the front door and walked in with 3 other team members, they searched the entire house and even tried to recreate what Rodney had seen but they were unable to recreate what he had seen; they concluded that what Rodney had seen was unexplainable.

Evidence and Conclusion

There was one piece of photographic evidence of an unexplained red orb, but no video evidence was captured. However, there were several EVPs captured. They heard the following EVP's and unexplained noises on their DVR's and microcassette recorder: an unexplained breath in the basement. In the entryway by phone BDPS captured two EVPs of an unexplained breath, 2 unexplained noises, a child's voice, footsteps heard by Scott and a low whispering of "No", an unexplained knock, unexplained knocks or hammering, a male voice saying, "Why", unexplained sounds on six different occasions, a very low whisper and unexplained whispering.

In the hallway by the kitchen the Following EVPs were captured: two unexplained sounds, a breath on three different occasions, an unexplained click, a female voice saying, "You should have known better to what", an unexplained growl, three more unexplained sounds (one of which Jeff heard), a possible gunshot and a beeping sound, and a very low whisper.

On live audio II the following was captured: a whispering of, "Hey, hey, hey" and then a noise and someone whispering, "Hi". In the upstairs hallway BDPS captured: a breath on three different occasions, a male whispering, "No", and six unexplained sounds (one of which sounded like a faint gunshot). And in the pink bedroom they captured someone whispering, "God", and a breath.

BDPS concluded that the client's home has high paranormal activity. The activity that helped BDPS to come to this determination were through the forms of EVP's, orb and personal experiences that helped us to determine our conclusion.

Case 049 Nickerson Snead Home 3/19/16

Case 049 Nickerson Snead Home 3/19/16

Case 049 Nickerson Snead Home 3/19/16

Case 049 Nickerson Snead Home 3/19/16

Sources

Archer, Bill. "Town to Temporarily Hold Cemetery Deeds." *Bluefield Daily Telegraph* barcher@bdtonline.com. Copyright © 1999-2008 cnhi, inc.

Blankenship, Paul Ray. "Massacre of Clay Children Remains an Infamous Episode." *The Wyoming County Report.*

Department of Sociology and Anthropology. Marshall University. Huntington, WV

Graham history has been provided by Nannie Tate Graham, local historians Davy Davis and Mary Kegley, Catherine S. McConnell *(Sanders Sage, 1972),* and by Frederick "Rick" Graham, grandson of Major David Graham, who passed away in 1990.
www.MajorGrahamMansion.com.

Hatche, T., Shrader, S., Nickols, A., Abel, M., Leslie, L., Pucket, C., and other members of the Tazewell County Historical Society. "The heritage of Tazewell county." va vol 2. *Tazewell County Historical Society.*

Horn, Dave. "The Midnight Ride of Molly Tynes."

Major Graham Mansion History Brochure

Mullins, Dr. Terry W. "Hidden Histories of Tazewell." *Quarrier Press.* Charleston, WV

O'Brien, C. "Barter Theatre." *Encyclopedia Virginia.* Virginia Foundation for the Humanities, 25 Feb. 2016. Web. 11 Aug. 2019.

UVA Anthropology Dept.

http://www.virginia.edu/anthropology/comments.html
Charlottesville, VA

UNC Anthropology Dept. Chapel Hill, NC

Virginia Tech Anthropology Dept. Department of History. Blacksburg, VA

ABOUT THE AUTHOR

Rodney Shortridge former/retired coal miner, printer and long-haul truck driver. Founded Black Diamond Paranormal Society (BDPS) 2008 and is lead investigator. Interviewed by local and national media on the paranormal. Appeared on A&E's Biography Channel "My Ghost Story" in 2011 interviewed about the Historic Pocahontas Cemetery and Major Grahma Mansion. Host of Within the Chaos on Blogtalkradio The Vibe Radio Network started 2016. Member of IMDb professional entertainment credits photographer, graphic artist, actor, executive producer, prop master, technical consultant, honorary entertainment, event speaker and artist. Founded Historic Pocahontas Haunted Walking Tours 2012-2016. Ex-Board Member of the Historic Pocahontas Inc. 2009-2016. Co-founder of Creative Photography Club 2011-2016. Founder of Creative Photo Club 2016. Founder and Sponsor of PhantomFest started 2018 to present. Member of paranomralsocieties.com, member of the haunting paranormal society network.

Rodney was born in Richlands, VA and raised in small town Rowe, VA, located in Buchannan County in the heart of the Appalachians. Wife Amy, four wonderful children, sons Aaron and Zackery daughters Lee and Dallas, and five grandchildren Half-pint, Hoss, Little Foot, Noah and JZ. His children and grandchildren are his life. His father died at the age of 46 and his passing was a tragic time in Rodney's life. Without his father's wisdom Rodney felt lost for many years until he realized he had to try to be the man his father wanted him to be for Rodney's own children. Rodney was diagnosed as being a Type 2 diabetic in 2002 and almost lost his life on 4 different occasions due to diabetes. Rodney has fought back and with the help of my family, friends, his doctors and nurses he has regained some of his health, but it is an everyday struggle. With the creation of Black Diamond Paranormal Society, Within the Chaos, Historic Pocahontas Haunted Walking Tours and PhantomFest it gives his life more meaning by being able to help and give back to so many people.

www.ingramcontent.com/pod-product-compliance
Lightning Source LLC
Chambersburg PA
CBHW051655040426
42446CB00009B/1140